Understanding the Science of Climate Change
Talking Points – Impacts to the Pacific Islands

Natural Resource Report NPS/NRPC/CCRP/NRR—2011/287

Amanda Schramm
National Park Service
Climate Change Response Program
1201 Oakridge Drive, Suite 200
Fort Collins, CO 80525

Rachel Loehman
Rocky Mountain Research Station
Fire Sciences Laboratory
5775 West US Hwy 10
Missoula, MT 59808-9361

With special thanks to the US Forest Service's Rocky Mountain Research Station and contributions from (in alphabetical order): Jeff Burgett, Darcy Hu, Fritz Klasner, Greg Kudray, Jade Moniz-Nakamura and Leigh Welling. Layout and design: Sara Melena, Angie Richman, Caitlin Shenk, and Katherine Stehli.

January 2011

U.S. Department of the Interior
National Park Service
Natural Resource Program Center
Fort Collins, Colorado

The Natural Resource Publication series addresses natural resource topics of interest and applicability to a broad readership in the National Park Service and to others in the management of natural resources, including the scientific community, the public, and the NPS conservation and environmental constituencies. Manuscripts are peer-reviewed to ensure the information is scientifically credible, technically accurate, appropriately written for the intended audience, and is designed and published in a professional manner.

Natural Resource Reports are the designated medium for disseminating high priority, current natural resource management information with managerial application. The series targets a general, diverse audience, and may contain NPS policy considerations or address sensitive issues of management applicability. Examples of the diverse array of reports published in this series include vital signs monitoring plans; monitoring protocols; "how to" resource management papers; proceedings of resource management workshops or conferences; annual reports of resource programs or divisions of the Natural Resource Program Center; resource action plans; fact sheets; and regularly-published newsletters.

Views, statements, findings, conclusions, recommendations and data in this report are solely those of the author(s) and do not necessarily reflect views and policies of the U.S. Department of the Interior, National Park Service. Mention of trade names or commercial products does not constitute endorsement or recommendation for use by the U.S. Government.

This report is available from the Natural Resource Publications Management website:
(http://www.nature.nps.gov/publications/NRPM)

Please cite this publication as:

Schramm, A and R. Loehman. 2011. Understanding the science of climate change: talking points - impacts to the Pacific Islands. Natural Resource Report NPS/NRPC/CCRP/NRR—2011/287. National Park Service, Fort Collins, Colorado.

NRInfo Reference URL: https://nrinfo.nps.gov/Reference.mvc/Profile?code=2167538

Climate Change Response Program webpage: http://www.nps.gov/climatechange/docs/PacificIslandsTP.pdf

Contents

Introduction 1

Climate Change Impacts to the Pacific Islands 2

   Summary..2

   List of Parks and Refuges 3

   Sectors:

      Temperature...4

      The Water Cycle 5

      Vegetation...8

      Wildlife 9

      Disturbance..13

      Cultural Resources 14

      Visitor Experience...16

No Regrets Actions 17

Global Climate Change.. 20

   Sectors:

      Temperature and greenhouse gases...20

      Water, Snow, and Ice...23

      Vegetation and Wildlife 25

      Disturbance..28

References 29

I. Introduction

Purpose

Climate change presents significant risks to our nation's natural and cultural resources. Although climate change was once believed to be a future problem, there is now unequivocal scientific evidence that our planet's climate system is warming (IPCC 2007a). While many people understand that human emissions of greenhouse gases have significantly contributed to recent observed climate changes, fewer are aware of the specific impacts these changes will bring. This document is part of a series of bio-regional summaries that provide key scientific findings about climate change and impacts to protected areas. The information is intended to provide a basic understanding of the science of climate change, known and expected impacts to resources and visitor experience, and actions that can be taken to mitigate and adapt to change. The statements may be used to communicate with managers, frame interpretive programs, and answer general questions from the public and the media. They also provide helpful information to consider in developing sustainability strategies and long-term management plans.

Audience

The Talking Points documents are primarily intended to provide park and refuge area managers and staff with accessible, up-to-date information about climate change and climate change impacts to the resources they protect.

Organizational Structure

Following the Introduction are three major sections of the document: a Regional Section that provides information on changes to the Pacific Islands, a section outlining No Regrets Actions that can be taken now to mitigate and adapt to climate changes, and a general section on Global Climate Change. The Regional Section is organized around seven types of changes or impacts, while the Global Section is arranged around four topics.

Regional Section

- Temperature
- The Water Cycle (including precipitation, snow, ice, and lake levels)
- Vegetation (plant cover, species range shifts, and phenology)
- Wildlife (aquatic and terrestrial animals, range shifts, invasive species, migration, and phenology)
- Disturbance (including range shifts, plant cover, plant pests and pathogens, fire, flooding, and erosion)
- Cultural Resources
- Visitor Experience

Global Section

- Temperature and Greenhouse Gases
- Water, Snow, and Ice
- Vegetation and Wildlife
- Disturbance

Information contained in this document is derived from the published results of a range of scientific research including historical data, empirical (observed) evidence, and model projections (which may use observed or theoretical relationships). While all of the statements are informed by science, not all statements carry the same level of confidence or scientific certainty. Identifying uncertainty is an important part of science but can be a major source of confusion for decision makers and the public. In the strictest sense, all scientific results carry some level of uncertainty because the scientific method can only "prove" a hypothesis to be false. However, in a practical world, society routinely elects to make choices and select options for actions that carry an array of uncertain outcomes.

The statements in this document have been organized to help managers and their staffs differentiate among current levels of uncertainty in climate change science. In doing so, the document aims to be consistent with the language and approach taken in the Fourth Assessment on Climate Change reports by the Intergovernmental Panel on Climate Change. However, this document discriminates among only three different levels of uncertainty and does not attempt to ascribe a specific probability to any particular level. These are qualitative rather than quantitative categories, ranked from greatest to least certainty, and are based on the following:

- "What scientists know" are statements based on measurable data and historical records. These are statements for which scientists generally have high confidence and agreement because they are based on actual measurements and observations. Events under this category have already happened or are very likely to happen in the future.

- "What scientists think is likely" represents statements beyond simple facts; these are derived from some level of reasoning or critical thinking. They result from projected trends, well tested climate or ecosystem models, or empirically observed relationships (statistical comparisons using existing data).

- "What scientists think is possible" are statements that use a higher degree of inference or deduction than the previous categories. These are based on research about processes that are less well understood, often involving dynamic interactions among climate and complex ecosystems. However, in some cases, these statements represent potential future conditions of greatest concern, because they may carry the greatest risk to protected area resources.

II. Climate Change Impacts to the Pacific Islands

The Pacific Islands bioregion discussed in this section is shown in the map to the right. A list of parks, refuges and sanctuaries for which this analysis is most useful is included on the next page. To help the reader navigate this section, each category is designated by color-coded tabs on the outside edge of the document.

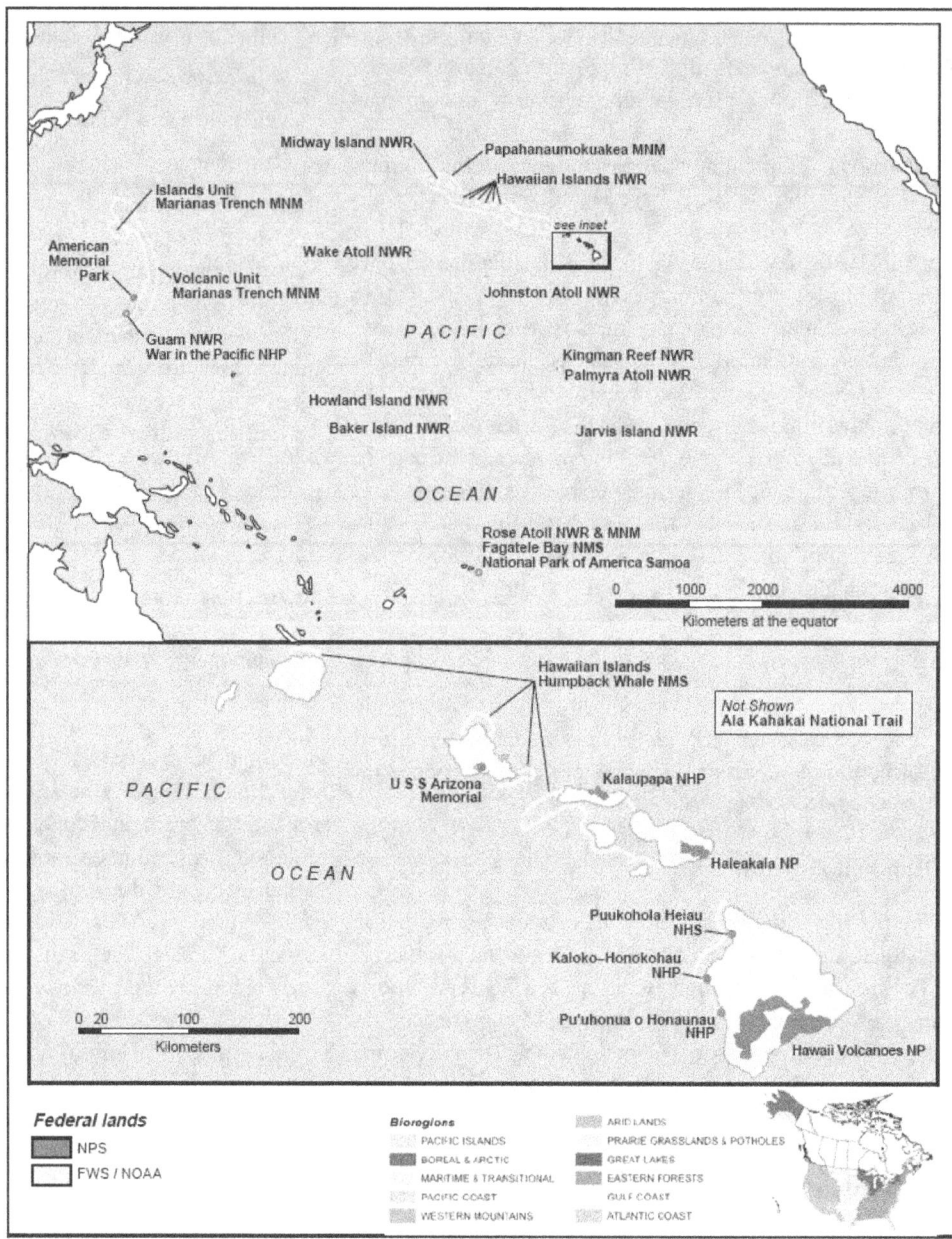

Temperature

Water Cycle

Vegetation

Wildlife

Disturbance

Cultural Resources

Visitor Experience

Summary

The Pacific islands face a variety of impacts as a result of climate change. Already-observed changes include increased average temperatures, coral bleaching, sea level rise and associated coastal erosion, increased intensity of cyclones, and a trend toward drier conditions. In the next century, sea level rise and associated erosion are expected to shrink shorelines and threaten human communities as well as species such as mangroves and endangered monk seals. Increased intensity of cyclones and storm surges could damage infrastructure, coastal habitat areas, and forests. High elevation cloud forests are projected to see reduced cloud cover and warmer temperatures that could facilitate the spread of diseases such as avian malaria, threatening endangered native birds like Hawaiian honeycreepers. Overall drier conditions and saltwater intrusion are expected to occur, straining fresh water supplies for irrigation and drinking water. Coral species will likely experience more frequent bleaching events due to higher sea surface temperatures, and many may die due to the effects of bleaching and decreasing oceanic pH (ocean acidification). Tourism and fisheries have high economic importance in this region, and both of these livelihoods are threatened by the predicted impacts to shorelines and marine ecosystems.

List of Parks, Refuges and Sanctuaries

U.S. National Park Service Units
- Ala Kahakai NHT
- American Memorial Park
- Haleakala NP
- Hawai'i Volcanoes NP
- Kalaupapa NHP
- Kaloko-Honokohau NHP
- National Park of American Samoa
- Pu'uhonua o Honaunau NHP
- Pu'ukohola Heiau NHS
- War in the Pacific NHP
- World War II Valor in the Pacific / USS Arizona Memorial

U.S. Fish & Wildlife Service Units
- Baker Island NWR
- Guam NWR
- Hakalau Forest NWR
- Hanalei NWR
- Howland Island NWR
- Huleia NWR
- James Campbell NWR
- Jarvis Island NWR
- Johnston Atoll NWR
- Kakahaia NWR
- Kealia Pond NWR
- Kilauea Point NWR
- Kingman Reef NWR
- Mariana Arc of Fire NWR
- Mariana Trench NWR
- Midway Atoll NWR
- O'ahu Forest NWR
- Palmyra Atoll NWR
- Pearl Harbor NWR
- Rose Atoll NWR
- Wake Atoll NWR

National Oceanic and Atmospheric Administration (NOAA) Marine National Monuments and Sanctuaries
- Fagatele Bay NMS
- Hawaiian Islands Humpback Whale NMS
- Marianas Trench MNM
- Pacific Remote Islands MNM
- Papahanaumokuakea MNM
- Rose Atoll MNM

Acronym	Unit Type
MNM	Marine National Monument
NHP	National Historical Park
NHS	National Historic Site
NHT	National Historic Trail
NMS	National Marine Sanctuary
NP	National Park
NWR	National Wildlife Refuge

A. Temperature

What scientists know....

- In the U.S. Pacific islands, average temperatures have risen by 0.5°F (0.28°C) during the past century (NABCI 2010).

- Temperature readings in Hawai'i over approximately the last 30 years show stronger warming at higher elevations and a relatively rapid rise in surface temperature (Giambelluca et al. 2008). The rate of temperature rise at low elevations (below 2600 feet) is 0.16°F (0.09°C)per decade, which is lower than the global rate of temperature increase; however, Hawai'i's rate of warming at high elevations is 0.48°F (0.27°C) per decade, which is faster than the global rate (ICAP 2010).

- The increase in mean temperature in Hawai'i is mostly due to a large increase in minimum temperatures rather than maximum temperatures. Minimum temperatures, including nighttime temperatures, have warmed about 3 times as much as maximum temperatures, resulting in a reduction of the daily temperature range (Giambelluca et al. 2008).

- Hawaiian waters have shown a warming trend over the past several decades. Average annual sea surface temperatures in Hawai'i have increased 0.8°C (1.44°F) since 1956 (Waddell and Clarke 2008).

This Remote Automated Weather Station (RAWS) at Kalaupapa National Historical Park can be used to measure temperature as well as other climactic factors; NPS photo.

- In American Samoa, the annual sea surface temperature only varies 2°C (3.6°F) on average - between about 27.5°C and 29.5°C (49.5°F and 53.1°F) - but warmer than normal sea surface temperatures have been observed in recent years (Waddell and Clarke 2008).

- In addition to a rise in sea surface temperature, the deep ocean (between 700 and 3,000 m, or about 2,300 to 9,000 feet) shows significant warming during the past several decades (Chen 2006; Fletcher 2009).

- The rise in average sea surface temperature has been accompanied by an increased frequency in El Niño-Southern Oscillation (ENSO) events (Bettencourt 2006).

What scientists think is likely....

- Warming in the western Pacific between 1993 and 2004 can largely be explained by significant warming of the ocean during the same period, which is likely linked to global warming (Chen 2006).

- Both air and ocean surface temperatures are expected to continue to increase in the Pacific (USGCRP 2009). Temperatures in the U.S. Pacific islands are expected to rise by an additional 4°F (2. 22°C) by 2090 (NABCI 2010).

- Studies of measured and modeled climate change effects that have been released since publication of the 2007 IPCC Fourth Assessment on Climate Change have shown that some of these effects, including sea surface temperature, rate of glacial melting, and sea level rise are likely even greater than predicted by the IPCC (Füssel 2009).

What scientists think is possible....

- Factoring in volcanic and solar activity and El Niño-Southern Oscillation events along with predictions of anthropogenic (human-caused) influences, modeling predicts that from 2009 to 2014, global temperature rises of about 0.15°C (0.27°F) could occur, a rate 50% greater than predicted by IPCC. However, the same models show that between 2014 and 2019, the

Temperature

Water Cycle

Vegetation

Wildlife

Disturbance

Cultural Resources

Visitor Experience

Projected sea-level rise on O'ahu by the year 2100. Photo copyright Coastal Geology Group: http://www.soest.hawaii.edu/coasts/sealevel/

Left margin tabs: Temperature, Water Cycle, Vegetation, Wildlife, Disturbance, Cultural Resources, Visitor Experience

B. THE WATER CYCLE

What scientists know....

• The state of Hawai'i has experienced a statewide decline in rainfall over the past two decades, coinciding with the mid-1970s climate change in the Pacific and associated changes in sea surface temperatures (Diaz et al. 2005). Historical trends have shown the number of heavy rainfall events decreasing across the Hawaiian Islands since 1905, based on average days of rainfall over 50mm (2 inches), over 10mm (0.4 inches), a simple daily intensity index, and average annual precipitation (Kruk and Levinson 2008). However, the amount of rain falling in the very heaviest downpours in Hawai'i (heaviest 1% of all events) increased approximately 12% between 1958 and 2007 (ICAP 2010).

• Solar radiation and net radiation measured at the summit of Haleakala, Maui, increased between 1990 and 2007, indicating decreased cloudiness (Giambelluca et al. 2008).

• Global mean sea level (GMSL) is estimated to be rising by approximately 3 mm/year (0.12 inches/year) (Fletcher 2009). Of the total rise in GMSL, a rise of between about 0.34 and 0.39 mm/year (0.014 and 0.014 inches/year) between 1955 and 2003 is attributable to steric effect (thermal expansion and salinity-density compensation of sea water) (Chen 2006).

• The current rate of sea level rise represents an acceleration compared to the average rate in the 20th century (Fletcher 2009). Similarly, the steric effect on sea level rise appears to have accelerated since the early 1990s (Chen 2006).

• Historical tide-gauge measurements show that the rates of global sea-level rise over the past 100 years are ten times greater than rates over the past 5,000 years (Field et al. 2008).

• The extent of sea level rise can differ from island to island. In Hawai'i, the varying geologic characteristics of the islands have resulted in sea level rise rates of 1.5 inches (3.8 cm) per decade on the Big Island,

rate of warming may slow (an increase of about 0.03°C, or 0.05°F) as a result of declining solar activity (Lean and Rind 2009).

• In the next 50 years, temperature and Carbon dioxide (CO_2) levels are predicted to increase beyond levels that coral reefs have experienced over the past half-million years (Hughes et al. 2003).

• The trend of warmer nighttime temperatures in Hawai'i could have serious negative impacts on vulnerable terrestrial ecosystems, where invasive species that are better adapted to warmer nighttime temperatures may out-compete native plants (Giambelluca et al. 2008).

• Hawai'i's air temperature trend used to closely follow the pattern of Pacific Decadal Oscillation events, which may be linked to sea surface temperature. In recent decades, however, air temperature trends have not closely followed local trends in ocean temperature, which may indicate an increasing influence of global warming on air temperature (Giambelluca et al. 2008).

about 1 inch (2.5 cm) per decade on Maui, and lower rates of about 0.6 inches (1.5 cm) per decade on O'ahu and Kauai due to the varying ages of the islands' underlying volcanic rock and associated levels of subsidence (Fletcher et al. 2002).

• Ocean areas with low surface chlorophyll are the least productive areas of the ocean. These areas expanded by about 15% between 1998 and 2006. A rise in mean sea surface temperature was experienced in the same areas during this period. Expansion of these low-chlorophyll areas is consistent with global warming models that predicted increasing stratification of ocean waters as sea surface temperatures rise, which would reduce ocean productivity. However, the rate of growth of these areas greatly exceeds previous predictions (Polovina et al. 2008).

• About 25% to 30% of anthropogenic (human-caused) carbon dioxide (CO_2) emissions in the atmosphere are absorbed by the earth's oceans, where the CO_2 reacts with the water to form carbonic acid in a process known as "ocean acidification" (Kleypas et al. 2006; Hoegh-Guldberg et al. 2007; Jokiel et al. 2008). The current and projected rate of CO_2 increase is about 100 times faster than has occurred over the past 650,000 years and the rising atmospheric CO_2 levels are irreversible on human timescales (Kleypas et al. 2006).

• The concentration of global atmospheric CO_2 has increased by about 35% since the preindustrial revolution, which has driven ocean pH from about 8.15 to 8.05 (a trend toward greater acidity). The lower pH corresponds with a 16% decrease in carbonate ion concentration, which is a building block for calcium carbonate (Kleypas 2006).

• Availability of calcium carbonate in ocean waters is essential for marine organisms like coral and pteropods (shell-building organisms) that use it for building their shells and calcium carbonate skeletons. Ocean acidification is resulting in a net loss of calcium carbonate saturation, which translates to slower calcification (inhibited reef-building capacity) and fast-

er dissolution for coral. This represents a major reversal of the previous trend of calcium carbonate increase in shallow-water ocean environments, which has been in effect worldwide for thousands of years (Kleypas et al. 1999; Orr et al. 2005; Andersson et al. 2009).

What scientists think is likely....

• Anomalous subsidence (cool air sinking) in Hadley cell wind circulation is likely partially responsible for the decline in Hawai'i's rainfall in recent decades (Diaz et al. 2005).

• A trend toward reduced precipitation in combination with a possible increase in evapotranspiration due to warmer temperatures would severely impact vulnerable high-elevation ecosystems by reducing ground-water recharge and stream discharge (Giambelluca et al. 2008).

• Warming climate will cause the peak wind intensities and near-storm precipitation from tropical cyclones to increase. Combined with sea-level rise, this is expected to cause higher storm surge levels. Frequent events such as these cause impacts to communities such as long-term deterioration of infrastructure, freshwater, and agricultural resources (USGCRP 2009).

• Hawai'i may experience a decline in fresh water resources and overall drier conditions while at the same time enduring more intense rainstorm events (ICAP 2010).

• Precipitation events in the Pacific are expected to shift from the normal winter rainy season to increased rainfall during summer months and increased frequency of heavy downpours. Increased summer rainfall is likely to result in increased flooding, which would reduce drinking water quality and crop yields (USGCRP 2009).

• Under most climate change scenarios, water resources on small islands will be severely compromised in the future due to changes in rainfall patterns and distribution (IPCC 2007). Long-term downward trends have been observed in base

Temperature

Water Cycle

Vegetation

Wildlife

Disturbance

Cultural Resources

Visitor Experience

Climate change is projected to result in increased tropical cyclone activity. This is a satellite image of Tropical Cyclone Ron, which hit the Pacific in 1998; NOAA photo.

flow of Hawaiian streams, corresponding to downward trends in rainfall. This may indicate a decline in ground-water storage and recharge, which has serious implications for drinking-water availability, because about 99 percent of domestic drinking water comes from groundwater. Lower stream base flows may also reduce water availability for other uses, particularly during periods of little or no rainfall, and may limit habitat availability for native stream fauna (Oki 2004).

- Impacts of sea level rise on Pacific Islands could include increased coastal erosion; increased frequency of flooding during high tides caused by storm events; and saltwater infiltration of the freshwater lens, which would affect the quality of drinking water supply (USGCRP 2009).

What scientists think is possible....

- Storm tracks that shift poleward in response to warming may be linked to a declining frequency of Hadley cell subsidence disruptions over Hawai'i. If this is a sign of long-term trends, the increasing frequency of trade wind inversions could be associated with a shift toward drier conditions that would affect Hawaiian mountainous tropical ecosystems and water resources (Cao et al. 2007).

- Modeling suggests that, based on the IPCC's Fourth Assessment Report A1B scenario (rapid economic growth, energy balanced across all sources), Hawai'i will experience a 5%–10% reduction of wet-season precipitation and a 5% increase of dry season precipitation by the end of the 21st century, as a result of changes in the wind field (Timm and Diaz 2009).

- Sea level is predicted to rise an additional 7 to 23 inches (17.5 to 57.5 cm) by the end of the 21st century due to thermal expansion, fresh water input and wind-driven effects, and to continue rising after the turn of the 22nd century (IPCC 2007).

- Ocean acidification is predicted to reduce oceanic pH by as much as 0.4 pH units by the end of this century. By 2050, ocean carbonate saturation levels may drop below the levels required to sustain coral reef building activity (Kleypas et al. 1999; Hoegh-Guldberg et al. 2007).

- The oceans may absorb as much as 90% of atmospheric CO_2 over the next millennium (Kleypas et al. 2006). Temperature-induced mass coral bleaching events resulting in wide geographic-scale coral death started when atmospheric CO_2 levels went over 320 parts per million (ppm). Levels today are closer to 387 ppm, which is expected to correlate to an irreversible decline for most reefs world-wide. Future projections predict annual mass bleaching events made worse by the effects of degraded water quality, increased severe weather events, and ocean acidification. If CO_2 levels reach 450 ppm (due to occur by 2030–2040 at current rates), reefs will face rapid decline world-wide, including extensive damage to shallow reef communities and reduction of biodiversity followed by extinctions. Reefs will cease to have most of their current value to human communities and will no longer be large-scale nursery grounds for fish. If CO_2 levels reach 600 ppm reefs will become eroding geological structures with surviving biotic populations restricted to limited refuges (Veron et al. 2009).

C. VEGETATION

What scientists know....

- Climate has demonstrably affected terrestrial ecosystems through changes in the seasonal timing of life-cycle events, plant growth responses (primary production), and biogeographic distribution (Parmesan 2006).

- In some high elevation island areas, warming has already led invasive species to overtake native species. Island forest areas are particularly at risk, as their relatively small areas are threatened not only by changes in temperature and precipitation, but also by increasingly violent storm events that have the ability to wipe out entire forests (IPCC 2007).

- Sea level rise poses a serious threat to mangroves. When the sea level rises faster than the underlying level of sediment, the mangroves can only find appropriate habitat by migrating landward, but limited suitable habitat is available to accommodate such a migration (Gilman et al. 2007; Gilman et al. 2008).

- The three largest mangrove forests in American Samoa (Masefau, Leone, and Nu'uuli) are obstructed from landward migration at a level of 16.5%, 23.4%, and 68.0%, respectively, due to human development. The observed landward migration of these mangroves over four decades was 12 to 37 times the observed relative sea-level rise rate (Gilman et al. 2006).

- Wetland kalo (taro) is cultivated throughout Hawai'i in order to be processed into poi, a popular staple food. Wetland kalo requires controlled irrigation to provide cool water flow to its roots for optimal crop health and productivity. Water temperature is the most critical physical factor in water use for kalo cultivation; the growing area must be kept adequately cool (at or below 25°C, or 77°F) throughout the growing cycle. When water temperatures are above the ideal temperature threshold, higher irrigation rates are needed to cool the system (Gingerich et al. 2007). Sea level rise and impacts to streamflow may also impact taro farming (ICAP 2010).

What scientists think is likely....

- Climate change poses a great threat to the future of cloud forests, as the areas experience intense storms; shifts in temperature, rainfall, and humidity; and other anticipated climate events. Some studies have already identified a decrease in low-elevation cloudiness in cloud forests. Optimum climatic conditions for cloud forest survival are expected to shift upwards in altitude by hundreds of meters by the time of CO_2 doubling. Such a shift would cause many cloud forests with narrow altitude ranges to be replaced by lower altitude ecosystems. The cloud forest ecosystems would experience biodiversity loss, altitude shifts in some species ranges, and extinction of high-elevation peak residing cloud forests (Foster 2001).

- Reduced mangrove area and health signifies a number of potential impacts to human safety, shoreline health, and eco-

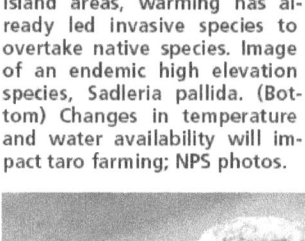

(Top) In some high elevation island areas, warming has already led invasive species to overtake native species. Image of an endemic high elevation species, Sadleria pallida. (Bottom) Changes in temperature and water availability will impact taro farming; NPS photos.

Temperature

Water Cycle

Vegetation

Wildlife

Disturbance

Cultural Resources

Visitor Experience

Temperature

Water Cycle

Vegetation

Wildlife

Disturbance

Cultural Resources

Visitor Experience

systems. Shorelines and adjacent communities would lose important protection from coastal hazards such as erosion, flooding, storm waves and surges, and tsunami. A loss of mangrove populations would also lead to reduced coastal water quality, less biodiversity, loss of fish and crustacean nursery habitat, and adverse impacts to adjacent coastal habitats (Gilman et al. 2008).

- The three largest mangrove forests in American Samoa (Masefau, Leone, and Nu'uuli) could experience as much as a 50% reduction in area by the year 2100. The Pacific Islands region as a whole could experience a 12% reduction in mangrove area by the year 2100 (Gilman et al. 2006).

What scientists think is possible....

- Experiments show that the effects of climate change on cloud forests could result in significant impacts to epiphytes (non-parasitic plants that grow on other plants, such as mosses, lichens, ferns, and bromeliads). Cloud forest epiphytes may experience decreased rates of growth and leaf production as well as increased mortality. As epiphytes die off, composition of canopy communities may undergo changes as terrestrial plants take over the remaining areas of arboreal soil (Nadkarni and Solano 2002).

- Human response to a significant increase or decrease in precipitation could have severe impacts to mangroves. Increased

groundwater extraction to compensate for reduced rainfall could exacerbate rates of sea level rise by lowering ground levels, increasing mangrove vulnerability. Conversely, an increase in rainfall could spur development of stormwater drainage systems that would divert surface water from mangroves and other coastal systems, reducing their productivity (Gilman et al. 2008).

- As seawalls are constructed to combat sea level rise and coastal erosion in island communities, adjacent mangroves immediately fronting and downcurrent from the structure will experience erosion and scouring (Gilman et al. 2008).

D. WILDLIFE

What scientists know....

- A meta-analysis of climate change effects on range boundaries in Northern Hemisphere species of birds, butterflies, and alpine herbs shows an average shift of 6.1 km (3.8 miles) per decade northward (or meters per decade upward), and a mean shift toward earlier onset of spring events (frog breeding, bird nesting, first flowering, tree budburst, and arrival of migrant butterflies and birds) of 2.3 days per decade (Parmesan and Yohe 2003).

- Erosion and loss of land area in the Northwestern Hawaiian Islands is reducing habitat for endangered monk seals that use this area for giving birth. Most of the islands at French Frigate Shoals were at least 50% smaller in 2004 than in 1963. Additional loss of land due to increasing frequency and intensity of storms, sea level rise, and other changes in oceanographic conditions will further threaten monk seal populations in this area (Antonelis et al. 2006). Monk seals have recently begun to re-colonize the main Hawaiian Islands and are showing some signs of success there (Baker and Johanos 2004).

- On the island of Hawai'i, incidence of malaria in forest birds has more than doubled over a decade, in correlation with warmer summer air temperatures and an increase in mosquito breeding (Freed et al. 2005).

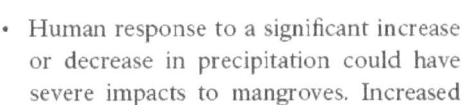

(Top) Warmer ocean temperatures cause heat-stressed corals to expel the beneficial algae that give them their brilliant color. Image of coral bleaching near Kalaupapa National Historical Park. (Bottom) Scientists survey coral near Kalaupapa National Historical Park; NPS photos.

Sea level rise and coastal erosion have removed some of the most important breeding grounds for the endangered monk seal; NPS photo.

- Studies have shown that a doubling in the partial pressure of CO_2 dissolved in the ocean's surface water corresponds to a 34% reduction in carbonate saturation state and a decrease in calcification rates ranging from 3% to 60% across a variety of benthic species and calcifying systems, with an average decline of 30% in corals. Other benthic species such as sea urchins and mollusks experience impaired growth and thinning of carbonate shells under increasingly acidic conditions (Kleypas et al. 2006).

- Coral recruitment, the process by which free-swimming coral larvae attach to hard surfaces and begin their development, has declined in parts of the Pacific. This indicates a decrease in corals' ability to recover from disturbance and replenish their populations through sexual reproduction (Waddell and Clarke 2008).

- Coral maintain a symbiotic relationship with beneficial algae that help to provide vital nutrients to the coral, and also lend them their brilliant colors. When ocean temperatures increase, the coral can become heat stressed, expelling these algae in a process referred to as "bleaching." Severe or prolonged thermal stress and resultant bleaching can lead to coral death (Hughes et al. 2003; Hoegh-Guldberg et al. 2007).

- Mass coral bleaching has increased in intensity and frequency in recent decades.

Corals may survive bleaching events and recover their symbiotic algae after mild thermal stress, but they may be more susceptible to coral disease and are likely to experience a reduction in growth, calcification, and fertility (Hoegh-Guldberg et al. 2007).

- In American Samoa, the Acropora, Millepora, and Porites coral colonies in shallow back reef pools have begun to bleach annually. This appears to be the first multispecies coral community in the world exhibiting annual summer mass bleaching (Waddell and Clarke 2008).

- Many shallow coral reefs throughout the Northwestern Hawaiian Islands experienced mass bleaching events in 2002 and 2004. In the 2004 event, colonies at numerous sites experienced death of nearly all surface-facing portions of coral, and overall coral mortality and algal overgrowth exceeded 50% at the three northern atolls (Kure, Pearl and Hermes, and Midway). A Porites compressa reef was heavily bleached in this event, and the dead coral skeletons were taken over by turf and macroalgae. This represents a major shift in the system, from one dominated by coral to one dominated by algae (Jokiel 2008; Waddell and Clarke 2008).

- Significant drops in coral cover were experienced at four of the six monitoring stations on Moloka'i between 2000 and 2004 (Field et al. 2008).

Temperature

Water Cycle

Vegetation

Wildlife

Disturbance

Cultural Resources

Visitor Experience

Temperature

Water Cycle

Vegetation

Wildlife

Disturbance

Cultural Resources

Visitor Experience

Birds like the Rota bridled white-eye in the Northern Mariana Islands (Top), and the Hawaiian honeycreepers like the 'I'iwi (Bottom) which make their home in high-elevation forests, face loss of habitat and the threat of avian malaria as temperatures rise; FWS photo (Top), NPS photo (Bottom).

What scientists think is likely....

- All 67 seabird species in U.S. waters are considered to have a medium or high vulnerability to climate change. Ninety-three percent of Hawaiian birds and 62% of all U.S. Pacific island birds exhibit medium or high vulnerability to climate change (NABCI 2010). In the Northwestern Hawaiian Islands, climate change and associated sea level rise are considered among the greatest threats to seabirds (Waddell and Clarke 2008).

- Due to their island endemism, reduced dispersal ability, and habitat exposure to the effects of climate change, 41 of the 42 native and endemic bird species of the Hawaiian Islands are considered severely threatened by climate change (NABCI 2010).

- Birds such as Puaiohi and 'Akiapōlā'au in Hawai'i and Rota Bridled White-eye in the Northern Mariana Islands, which live mainly in high-elevation forests, will be threatened by rising temperatures. Species such as Laysan Duck and Laysan Finch in Hawai'i will lose habitat due to sea level rise. Coastal forests important to the Micronesian Megapode in Northern Mariana Islands may also be threatened by rising sea levels (Benning et al. 2002; NABCI 2010).

- High-elevation populations of Hawaiian honeycreepers, Hawai'i's most endangered birds, may be at increased risk of avian disease as temperatures warm and disease vectors (such as mosquitoes) become present and viable in areas that are currently out of their range (Atkinson and LaPointe 2009). Increase in forest temperature due to climate change, in combination with land use changes and spread of avian disease, is likely to drive several of the remaining species of Hawaiian honeycreepers to extinction, especially on the islands of Kauai and Hawai'i (Benning et al. 2002).

- Pacific tuna populations are expected to decline and to shift eastward as ocean temperatures warm (USGCRP 2009).

- Echinoderms such as sea stars, sea cucumbers, and sea urchins have bodies that are largely made up of calcium carbonate, and their populations capture an estimated 0.1 gigatons of carbon per year from oceans worldwide. These species may be highly susceptible to ocean acidification, with effects such as failure of recruitment of planktonic larvae, larval death, and impairments to growth and development (Lebrato et al. 2009: preprint).

- Increases in sea surface temperature and reductions in ocean carbonate levels are such that essentially all present-day reef habitats in the Pacific Ocean will be "marginal" (pushed beyond their "normal" environmental limits) within the next several decades. Regions of high temperature and low carbonate saturation state will be subject to a combination of conditions that has probably not occurred in evolutionary history (Guinotte et al. 2003).

- The rate of atmospheric CO_2 change is a critical factor for the future health of coral, because modern corals do not appear to have the capacity to adapt quickly to sudden environmental change. Recent and future projected rates of change are more extreme than the ice age transitions by orders of magnitude. Given the dramatic shifts in biology at specific locations during those events, it is likely that future changes will exceed the adaptive capacity of most organisms (Hoegh-Guldberg et al. 2007).

- Observations of coral bleaching in Guam in recent years coincided with elevated sea surface temperature, and suggest that bleaching events may become increasingly frequent and severe (Burdick et al. 2008).

- Hawaiian coral reefs will be increasingly vulnerable to large-scale bleaching if the current trend of increasing temperatures continues. Shallow areas with little water circulation will be most affected and will likely experience increased mortality, while open coastal areas adjacent to deep oceanic water are likely to be the last affected (Jokiel and Brown 2004).

- Experimental evidence shows that ocean acidification has a profound impact on the development and growth of crustose coralline algae (CCA) populations. If the current trends of ocean acidification and decline of ocean carbonate continue, marine organisms such as corals, crustose coralline algae (CCA), and plankton will have difficulty building and maintaining their shells and calcium carbonate skeletons (Orr et al. 2005; Kleypas et al. 2006; Jokiel et al. 2008).

- When ocean acidification predicted by the end of the 21st century under the IPCC "business as usual" scenario (IS92a) was approximated in experimental conditions, growth of CCA in the acidified water experienced an 86% relative reduction compared to the non-acidified samples. Rhodoliths, a type of CCA, showed a 250% decrease compared to the controls, changing from positive to negative accretion (growth) in the acidified water. This same experiment demonstrated a reduction in coral calcification between 15% and 20% and a decrease in linear extension by 14% under acidified conditions. Some coral species (Pocillopora damicornis and Montipora capitata) were able to reproduce under the acidified conditions. (Jokiel et al. 2008).

What scientists think is possible....

- The synergism of rapid temperature rise and stresses such as habitat destruction may disrupt connectedness among species, lead to reformulation of species communities, and result in numerous extirpations and/or extinctions (Root et al. 2003).

Coral reefs and carbonate-dependent species like the Crown-of-thorns starfish could lose the ability to form their calcium carbonate skeletons as carbonate content decreases in acidifying ocean waters; NPS photo.

- A 2°C (3.6°F) rise in average regional temperature could cause Hanawi Natural Area Reserve on Maui to lose 57% of its remaining low-risk area for avian malaria, increasing the risk of infection to endangered Maui Parrotbill and Ākohekohe. On Kaua'i and O'ahu, all forested areas are prone to some level of malaria transmission due to warm temperatures; however, warming on Kaua'i would result in an 85% decrease in the area where transmission is currently limited and seasonal, which would increase risk for already-vulnerable species such as 'Akeke'e and 'Akikiki, and could lead to further declines in their populations (Benning et al. 2002).

- By the year 2100, projected reductions in land area in the Northwestern Hawaiian Islands due to sea level rise and spring tide inundations would result in significant habitat loss that would impact endangered Hawaiian monk seals, threatened Hawaiian green sea turtles, and the endangered Laysan finch at Pearl and Hermes Reef. After 2100, sea level rise will continue to increase, resulting in further loss of land area and associated breeding habitat for these same species at atolls such as French Frigate Shoals and Pearl and Hermes Reef, where the majority of land is currently less than 2 m above sea level (Baker et al. 2006).

- Modeling shows that a warming climate could increase populations of the invasive frog species Eleutherodactylus coqui in the Pacific Islands, expanding to higher elevations in the Hawaiian Islands in particular. Densities of this species on the island of Hawai'i are currently the highest in the world (RÖdder 2009).

- A high degree of seasonal sea surface temperature fluctuation may be associated with increased level of coral disease (Aeby 2007).

- Scientists believe that coral bleaching can slow or stop growth, and coral populations that experience annual bleaching are probably growing less than unbleached corals. Bleaching has also been found to block sexual reproduction of coral for a year, which means that corals that bleach annually can only reproduce asexually, by fragmentation (Waddell and Clarke 2008).

Temperature

Water Cycle

Vegetation

Wildlife

Disturbance

Cultural Resources

Visitor Experience

Temperature

Water Cycle

Vegetation

Wildlife

Disturbance

Cultural Resources

Visitor Experience

Damage at War in the Pacific National Historical Park from 2002's Typhoon Pongsona; NPS photos.

- Moloka'i has the longest contiguous coral reef tract in the main Hawaiian Islands, but changes to sea level and climate are expected to further exacerbate stresses to the reef system, and potentially lead to its demise (Field et al. 2008).

- Almost 60% of the world's coral reefs may be lost by 2030, and an estimated 30% of coral reefs worldwide are already severely damaged. There are no coral reefs left that are considered pristine (Hughes et al. 2003). If current carbon dioxide emission trends continue, ocean acidification will become intense enough that corals will not survive this century (Caldeira 2007).

E. DISTURBANCE

What scientists know....

- Flooding from sea-level rise and storm events can impact infrastructure such as roads, bridges, harbors, port facilities, and airports, sometimes requiring closure of facilities (USGCRP 2009).

- The number of Pacific Islanders affected by extreme weather events such as cyclones, floods, and droughts has increased dramatically in recent decades (Finucane 2009).

- Cyclones have become increasingly intense in the past 30 years, corresponding to an increase in significant wave heights (Bettencourt 2006). There has been an increasing tendency toward intense hurricanes in the western Pacific and a decreasing tendency in the eastern Pacific since the 1980s. Increasing sea surface temperature is a critical factor for intense hurricanes (CCSP 2008).

- A coastal vulnerability assessment of 22 coastal national parks found that Pacific Island parks are moderately vulnerable to sea level rise. Mean sea-level rise rates were calculated at 0.10 mm/year at War In The Pacific National Monument in Guam, 1.48 mm/year at the National Park of American Samoa, and 3.36mm/year at Kaloko-Honokohau National Historical Park in Hawai'i (Pendleton et al. 2010).

- In September 2003, the harbor in Honolulu, Hawai'i experienced the highest daily average sea level ever recorded as the result of a combination of long-term sea-level rise, normal seasonal heating and high tide events, and an ocean circulation event that temporarily raised local sea level. Extreme events such as these are occurring more frequently as average sea level rises, shifting from an historic interval of every 20 years to approximately every 5 years (USGCRP 2009).

What scientists think is likely....

- Islands are considered uniquely vulnerable to the effects of climate change due to their limited size and their proneness to natural hazards and external shocks. Islands also often have low adaptive capacity and high adaptive costs relative to gross domestic product (GDP) (IPCC 2007).

- Rising sea levels are expected to exacerbate inundation, storm surge, erosion and other coastal hazards, which will threaten vital infrastructure, facilities, human settlements, and the livelihood of island communities. This may be particularly pronounced in the Pacific, where reductions in island size may be severe, and where more than 50% of the population currently lives within 1.5 km of the shore (IPCC 2007).

- Low-lying, low relief, and low slope coasts that are susceptible to erosion will be the most vulnerable to impacts from rising sea levels. The shorelines of Oʻahu and Kauai are predicted to retreat 4-5 feet per decade (Fletcher et al. 2002).

- A decline in the health of coral reef systems will expose shorelines to increased impacts from waves and storms that are currently buffered by the healthy coral communities. This will signify increased vulnerability for human communities and infrastructure, as well as lagoon and estuarine ecosystems, including mangroves, seagrass meadows, and salt marshes (Hoegh-Guldberg et al. 2007).

- Heavier rainfall events will likely result in flash floods, mudslides, and damage to infrastructure (ICAP 2010).

- Managaha, a small sand cay in Saipan Lagoon in the Northern Mariana Islands, has experienced a rapid rate of erosion from its northeast shore and accretion on the west since 1996. Sea level rise in this area will exacerbate this trend, threatening shearwater bird nesting habitat (Waddell and Clarke 2008).

- Ocean acidification has caused a decrease in sound absorption. Based on current projections of future pH values for the oceans, a decrease in sound absorption of 40% is expected by mid-century, resulting in increased ocean noise within the critical auditory range for environmental, military, and economic interests, and with unknown implications for acoustically sensitive marine mammals (Hester et al. 2008).

What scientists think is possible....

- Climate models project an increased frequency of tropical cyclones in the western North Pacific due to global warming (Emanuel et al. 2007). The intensity of cyclones in the Pacific is expected to increase by 5% to 20% by the end of the 21st Century (Bettencourt 2006).

- In tropical oceans, heat stress caused by warmer summer temperatures may increase susceptibility to disease (Harvell et al. 2002).

- By the year 2100, sea level rise in the Northwestern Hawaiian Islands is expected to result in a land area reduction of 3% to 65% under a median scenario and 5% to 75% under the maximum scenario. All land below 89 cm (34.7 inches) under the median scenario and 129 cm (50.3 inches) under the maximum scenario in elevation would likely be inundated periodically by Spring tides (Baker et al. 2006).

F. CULTURAL RESOURCES

- Coastal archeological sites are threatened by erosion and storm surges. Coastal cyclonic activity has been known to destroy entire archeological assemblages and to rework coastal midden areas (Spennemann 2004).

- Pelakane Beach and Ala Kahakai NHT in Puʻukoholā Heiau National Historic Site have been identified as threatened by sea level rise. At Kaloko-Honokōhau National Historical Park, Kaloko Seawall, the beach fronting ʻAimakapā Fishpond, and ʻAiʻōpio Fishtrap are at greatest risk of deterioration due to coastal impacts (Vitousek et al. 2009). The Kaloko seawall protects important cultural resources, including outstanding examples of native

Traditional fishing with a basket fish trap. Fishing is an integral part of Pacific Island culture, and the health of fisheries is threatened by deteriorating coral reefs and changing ocean conditions; NPS photo.

The historic fish ponds at Kaloko-Honokohau National Historical Park are threatened by sea level rise; NPS photo.

Hawaiian culture and religious sites, but would be inadequate with a sea level rise of 1.5 feet (Saunders 2009).

• Both subsistence and commercial agriculture on small islands are threatened by the effects of climate change, including changes in temperature and precipitation as well as sea level rise and sea water intrusion into freshwater systems (IPCC 2007).

• The small communities and economies of the Pacific Islands are particularly vulnerable to natural hazards and the impacts of climate change due to their high level of dependence on natural resources (Anderson 2009).

• Climate impacts in the Pacific are linked with socioeconomic stresses such as relocation of coastal communities, deteriorating infrastructure, and threats to tourism, agriculture, and other major economic elements (Finucane 2009).

• As coral reef health declines due to climate impacts, the density of reef fish is likely to decrease, threatening all types of reef-based fisheries, including subsistence, industrial, and those that supply the aquarium trade (Hoegh-Guldberg et al. 2007).

• Coral reefs provide economic benefits to islands by supporting fisheries, drawing tourism, providing scientific and educational value, contributing to biodiversity, and protecting shorelines against wave

erosion. The net economic benefits of coral reefs for Hawai'i are estimated at $360 million annually, with the overall asset value conservatively estimated at nearly $10 billion (Cesar and van Beukering 2004; Hoegh-Guldberg et al. 2007; USGCRP 2009).

• Coral resources in Guam have significant roles in the economy and culture of the island. The economic value of coral reef resources is estimated at approximately $127 million per year. Coral reefs serve a variety of functions for Guam's residents, including cultural and traditional use, tourism, recreation, fisheries, and shoreline and infrastructure protection (Waddell and Clarke 2008).

• Large-scale climate shifts are linked to "regime shifts," or changes in local ecosystem composition, for fisheries. This poses a challenge for fisheries managers who rely on a fixed harvest rate. As climate change results in shifts to fish species availability, fisheries will have to adapt their management strategies to the new conditions (Polovina 2005).

• Reduced fish availability could have serious impacts for both fisheries and the diet of native communities. Most communities in the Pacific Islands derive between 25% and 69% percent of their animal protein from fish (USGCRP 2009).

• Declines in tuna availability will impact Pacific Island food availability and challenge economies that rely on fishing or canning. Local canneries in places like American Samoa are also culturally important as large-scale employers of women, and an important factor in maintaining gender equity (Lal et al. 2009; USGCRP 2009).

• An increase in population of the invasive frog species Eleutherodactylus coqui in the Pacific Islands has economic implications for floraculture, a multi-million-dollar industry. In Guam and Hawai'i, accidental transport and spread of this species has already occurred through the trade of plants and flowers, and quarantine restrictions and de-infestation measures are now required before potentially exposed plants can be exported (RÖdder 2009).

- A reduction or decline in health of Mangrove populations could have major economic impacts for some Pacific Island communities. Mangroves represent a major resource for communities that rely on them for numerous products and services. The annual economic value of mangroves is estimated to be $200,000 to $900,000 per hectare (Gilman et al. 2008).

- Benefits of using local knowledge and traditional practices in resource management can help facilitate adaptation to climate change (Finucane 2009).

G. VISITOR EXPERIENCE

- The locations of climatically ideal tourism conditions are likely to shift toward higher latitudes under projected climate change, as a consequence redistribution in the locations and seasons of tourism activities may occur. The effects of these changes will depend greatly on the flexibility of institutions and tourists as they react to climate change (Amelung et al. 2007).

- Climate change is expected to have both direct and indirect effects on tourism on small islands, most of which are negative. Eroded beaches, degradation and bleaching of coral reefs, and a loss of cultural heritage from inundation and flooding would reduce the amenity value of coastal areas. Water shortages and potential increases in vectorborne diseases may also deter tourists. Warmer temperatures may make some areas (low-latitude islands) unappealing, while increasing the appeal of others (mid- to high-latitude islands) (IPCC 2007).

- Tourism to the Pacific Islands could be negatively affected by climate-related impacts to infrastructure, freshwater quality and availability, public health concerns about diseases, erosion of beaches, and destruction of natural resources that attract visitors, such as coral reefs and mangroves. This could have significant impacts on islands like Hawai'i whose economies rely on strong tourism revenues (Hoegh-Guldberg et al. 2007; USGCRP 2009).

- Over one million Asian tourists visit Guam each year. Tourism accounts for 20% of Guam's GDP (32% of non-governmental GDP) and provides over 15,000 direct and indirect jobs to residents. The health of coral ecosystems is directly linked to Guam's tourism, as the beauty of the reefs and the protection that they provide for inshore recreational activities help attract visitors. The Guam Coral Reef Initiative Coordinating Committee identified climate change as one of the top five priority threats impacting Guam's coral reefs (Waddell and Clarke 2008).

- Increased populations of the invasive frog species Eleutherodactylus coqui in the Pacific Islands could cause major noise disturbances that would affect visitor experience. The frog's loud, piercing call is already a nuisance to residents and hotel guests in some island areas, and has elicited complaints, affected property values, and even led to declaration of a noise-related state of emergency in Hilo in 2004 (RÖdder 2009).

Visitors stroll along a beach at the National Park of American Samoa. Tourism is an important part of the economy in the Pacific Islands, and is partly dependent on the health and attractiveness of the islands' beaches and coral reefs; NPS photo.

Temperature

Water Cycle

Vegetation

Wildlife

Disturbance

Cultural Resources

Visitor Experience

III. No Regrets Actions: How Individuals, Parks, Refuges, and Their Partners Can Do Their Part

Individuals, businesses, and agencies release carbon dioxide (CO_2), the principal greenhouse gas, through burning of fossil fuels for electricity, heating, transportation, food production, and other day-to-day activities. Increasing levels of atmospheric CO_2 have measurably increased global average temperatures, and are projected to cause further changes in global climate, with severe implications for vegetation, wildlife, oceans, water resources, and human populations. Emissions reduction – limiting production of CO_2 and other greenhouse gases - is an important step in addressing climate change. It is the responsibility of agencies and individuals to find ways to reduce greenhouse gas emissions and to educate about the causes and consequences of climate change, and ways in which we can reduce our impacts on natural resources. There are many simple actions that each of us can take to reduce our daily carbon emissions, some of which will even save money.

Agencies Can...

Improve sustainability and energy efficiency

- Use energy efficient products, such as ENERGY STAR® approved office equipment and light bulbs.

- Initiate an energy efficiency program to monitor energy use in buildings. Provide guidelines for reducing energy consumption. Conserve water.

- Convert to renewable energy sources such as solar or wind generated power.

- Specify "green" designs for construction of new or remodeled buildings.

- Include discussions of climate change in the park Environmental Management System.

- Conduct an emissions inventory and set goals for CO_2 reduction.

- Provide alternative transportation options such as employee bicycles and shuttles for within-unit commuting.

- Provide hybrid electric or propane-fueled vehicles for official use, and impose fuel standards for park vehicles. Reduce the number and/or size of park vehicles and boats to maximize efficiency.

- Provide a shuttle service or another form of alternate transportation for visitor and employee travel to and within the unit.

- Provide incentives for use of alternative transportation methods.

- Use teleconferences and webinars or other forms of modern technology in place of travel to conferences and meetings.

Implement Management Actions

- Engage and enlist collaborator support (e.g., tribes, nearby agencies, private landholders) in climate change discussions, responses, adaptation and mitigation.

- Develop strategies and identify priorities for managing uncertainty surrounding climate change effects in parks and refuges.

- Dedicate funds not only to sustainable actions but also to understanding the impacts to the natural and cultural resources.

- Build a strong partnership-based foundation for future conservation efforts.

- Identify strategic priorities for climate change efforts when working with partners.

- Incorporate anticipated climate change impacts, such as decreases in lake levels or changes in vegetation and wildlife, into management plans.

An interpretive brochure about climate change impacts to National Parks was created in 2006 and was distributed widely. This brochure was updated in 2008.

Climate Change in National Parks

Park Service employees install solar panels at San Francisco Maritime National Historical Park (Top); At the National Mall, Park Service employees use clean-energy transportation to lead tours; NPS photos.

flows for fish, and maintain and develop access corridors to climate change refugia.

- Restoration efforts are important as a means for enhancing species' ability to cope with stresses and adapt to climatic and environmental changes. Through restoration of natural areas, we can lessen climate change impacts on species and their habitats. These efforts will help preserve biodiversity, natural resources, and recreational opportunities.

- Address climate change impacts to cultural resources by taking actions to document, preserve, and recover them.

Educate staff and the public

- Post climate change information in easily accessible locations such as on bulletin boards and websites.

- Provide training for park and refuge employees and partners on effects of climate change on resources, and on dissemination of climate change knowledge to the public.

- Support the development of region, park, or refuge-specific interpretive products on the impacts of climate change.

- Incorporate climate change research and information in interpretive and education outreach programming.

- Distribute up-to-date interpretive products (e.g., the National Park Service-wide Climate Change in National Parks brochure).

- Develop climate change presentations for local civic organizations, user and partner conferences, national meetings, etc.

- Incorporate climate change questions and answers into Junior Ranger programs.

- Help visitors make the connection between reducing greenhouse gas emissions and resource stewardship.

- Encourage visitors to use public or non-motorized transportation to and around parks.

- Encourage climate change research and scientific study in park units and refuges.

- Design long-term monitoring projects and management activities that do not rely solely on fossil fuel-based transportation and infrastructure.

- Incorporate products and services that address climate change in the development of all interpretive and management plans.

- Take inventory of the facilities/boundaries/species within your park or refuge that may benefit from climate change mitigation or adaptation activities.

- Participate in gateway community sustainability efforts.

- Recognize the value of ecosystem services that an area can provide, and manage the area to sustain these services. Conservation is more cost-effective than restoration and helps maintain ecosystem integrity.

- Provide recycling options for solid waste and trash generated within the park.

Restore damaged landscapes

- Strategically focus restoration efforts, both in terms of the types of restoration undertaken and their national, regional, and local scale and focus, to help maximize resilience.

- Restore and conserve connectivity within habitats, protect and enhance instream

> "Humankind has not woven the web of life. We are but one thread within it. Whatever we do to the web, we do to ourselves. All things are bound together. All things connect."
> —Chief Seattle

- Encourage visitors to reduce their carbon footprint in their daily lives and as part of their tourism experience.

Individuals can...

- In the park or refuge park their car and walk or bike. Use shuttles where available. Recycle and use refillable water bottles. Stay on marked trails to help further ecosystem restoration efforts.

- At home, walk, carpool, bike or use public transportation if possible. A full bus equates to 40 fewer cars on the road. When driving, use a fuel-efficient vehicle.

- Do not let cars or boats idle - letting a car idle for just 20 seconds burns more gasoline than turning it off and on again.

- Replace incandescent bulbs in five most frequently used light fixtures in the home with bulbs that have the ENERGY STAR® rating. If every household in the U.S. takes this one action we will prevent greenhouse gas emissions equivalent to the emissions from nearly 10 million cars, in addition to saving money on energy costs.

Reduce, Reuse, Recycle, Refuse

- Use products made from recycled paper, plastics and aluminum - these use 55-95% less energy than products made from scratch.

- Purchase a travel coffee mug and a reusable water bottle to reduce use of disposable products (Starbucks uses more than 1 billion paper cups a year).

- Carry reusable bags instead of using paper or plastic bags.

- Recycle drink containers, paper, newspapers, electronics, and other materials. Bring recyclables home for proper disposal when recycle bins are not available. Rather than taking old furniture and clothes to the dump, consider "recycling" them at a thrift store.

- Keep an energy efficient home. Purchase ENERGY STAR® appliances, properly insulate windows, doors and attics, and lower the thermostat in the winter and raise it in the summer (even 1-2 degrees makes a big difference). Switch to green power generated from renewable energy sources such as wind, solar, or geothermal.

- Buy local goods and services that minimize emissions associated with transportation.

- Encourage others to participate in the actions listed above.

- Conserve water.

For more information on how you can reduce carbon emissions and engage in climate-friendly activities, check out these websites:

EPA- What you can do: http://www.epa.gov/climatechange/wycd/index.html

NPS- Climate Change Response Program: http://www.nps.gov/climatechange

NPS- Do Your Part! Program: http://www.nps.gov/climatefriendlyparks/doyourpart.html

US Forest Service Climate Change Program: http://www.fs.fed.us/climatechange/

United States Global Change Research Program: http://www.globalchange.gov/

U.S. Fish and Wildlife Service Climate change: http://www.fws.gov/home/climatechange/

The Climate Friendly Parks Program is a joint partnership between the U.S. Environmental Protection Agency and the National Park Service. Climate Friendly Parks from around the country are leading the way in the effort to protect our parks' natural and cultural resources and ensure their preservation for future generations; NPS image.

IV. Global Climate Change

The IPCC is a scientific intergovernmental, international body established by the World Meteorological Organization (WMO) and by the United Nations Environment Programme (UNEP). The information the IPCC provides in its reports is based on scientific evidence and reflects existing consensus viewpoints within the scientific community. The comprehensiveness of the scientific content is achieved through contributions from experts in all regions of the world and all relevant disciplines including, where appropriately documented, industry literature and traditional practices, and a two stage review process by experts and governments.

Definition of climate change: The IPCC defines climate change as a change in the state of the climate that can be identified (e.g. using statistical tests) by changes in the mean and/or the variability of its properties, and that persists for an extended period, typically decades or longer. All statements in this section are synthesized from the IPCC report unless otherwise noted.

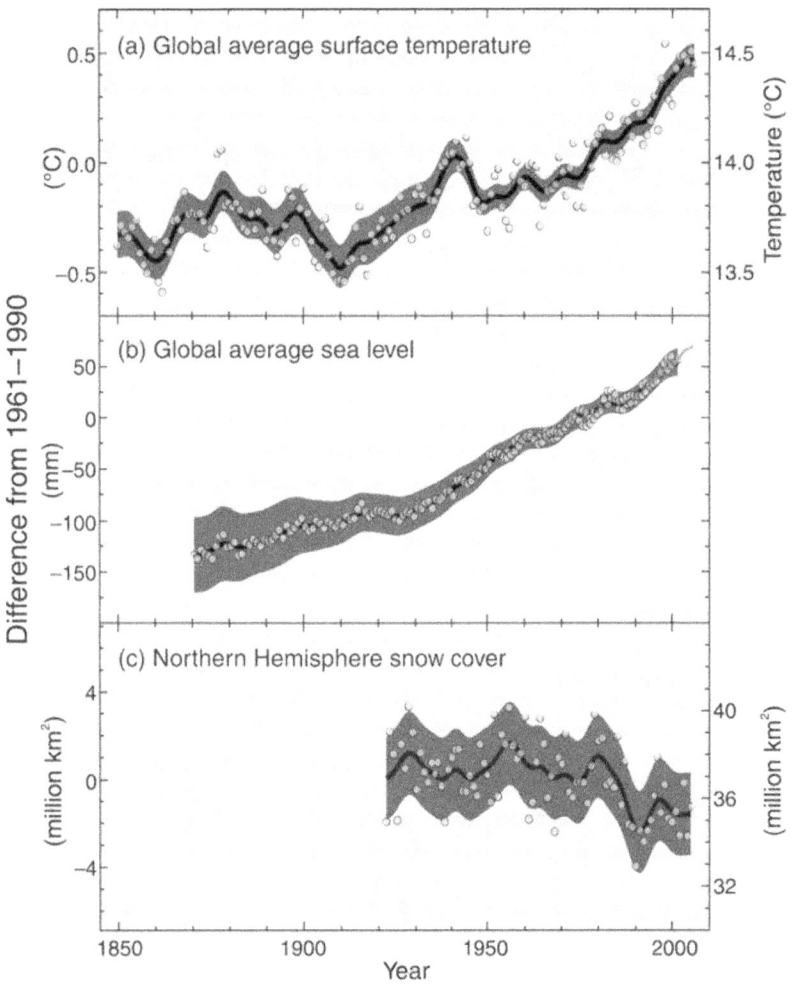

Figure 1. Observed changes in (a) global average surface temperature; (b) global average sea level from tide gauge (blue) and satellite (red) data and (c) Northern Hemisphere snow cover for March-April. All differences are relative to corresponding averages for the period 1961-1990. Smoothed curves represent decadal averaged values while circles show yearly values. The shaded areas are the uncertainty intervals estimated from a comprehensive analysis of known uncertainties (a and b) and from the time series (c) (IPCC 2007a).

A. Temperature and Greenhouse Gases

What scientists know...

- Warming of the Earth's climate system is unequivocal, as evidenced from increased air and ocean temperatures, widespread melting of snow and ice, and rising global average sea level (Figure 1).

- In the last 100 years, global average surface temperature has risen about 0.74°C over the previous 100-year period, and the rate of warming has doubled from the previous century. Eleven of the 12 warmest years in the instrumental record of global surface temperature since 1850 have occurred since 1995 (Figure 1).

- Although most regions over the globe have experienced warming, there are regional variations: land regions have warmed faster than oceans and high northern latitudes have warmed faster than the tropics. Average Arctic temperatures have increased at almost twice the global rate in the past 100 years, primarily because loss of snow and ice results in a positive feedback via increased absorption of sunlight by ocean waters (Figure 2).

- Over the past 50 years widespread changes in extreme temperatures have been observed, including a decrease in cold days and nights and an increase in the frequency of hot days, hot nights, and heat waves.

- Winter temperatures are increasing more rapidly than summer temperatures, particularly in the northern hemisphere, and

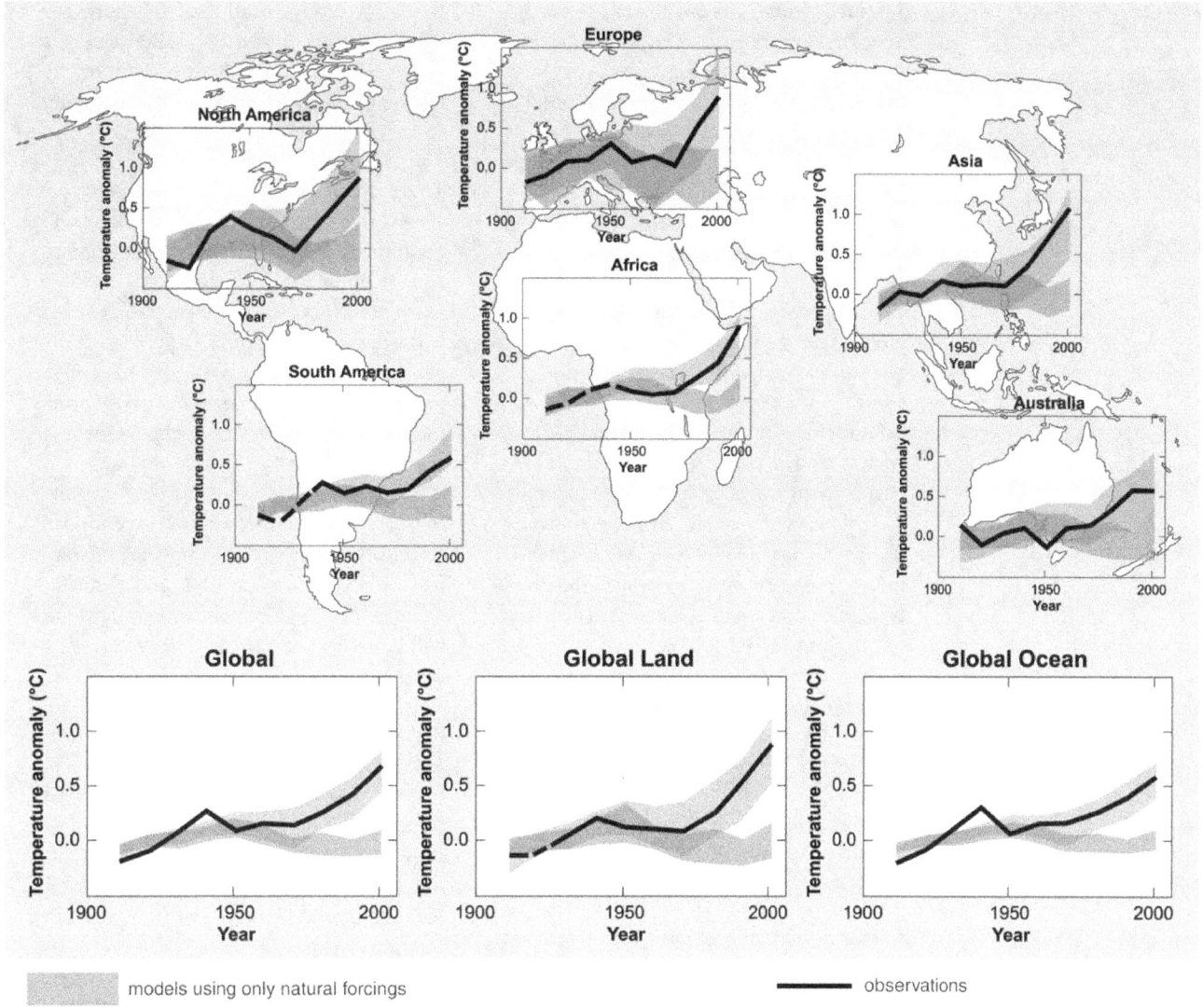

models using only natural forcings

models using both natural and anthropogenic forcings

observations

Figure 2. Comparison of observed continental- and global-scale changes in surface temperature with results simulated by climate models using either natural or both natural and anthropogenic forcings. Decadal averages of observations are shown for the period 1906-2005 (black line) plotted against the centre of the decade and relative to the corresponding average for the period 1901-1950. Lines are dashed where spatial coverage is less than 50%. Blue shaded bands show the 5 to 95% range for 19 simulations from five climate models using only the natural forcings due to solar activity and volcanoes. Red shaded bands show the 5 to 95% range for 58 simulations from 14 climate models using both natural and anthropogenic forcings (IPCC 2007a).

there has been an increase in the length of the frost-free period in mid- and high-latitude regions of both hemispheres.

• Climate change is caused by alterations in the energy balance within the atmosphere and at the Earth's surface. Factors that affect Earth's energy balance are the atmospheric concentrations of greenhouse gases and aerosols, land surface properties, and solar radiation.

• Global atmospheric concentrations of greenhouse gases have increased significantly since 1750 as the result of human activities. The principal greenhouse gases are carbon dioxide (CO_2), primarily from fossil fuel use and land-use change; methane (CH_4) and nitrous oxide (N_2O), primarily from agriculture; and halocarbons

(a group of gases containing fluorine, chlorine or bromine), principally engineered chemicals that do not occur naturally.

• Direct measurements of gases trapped in ice cores demonstrate that current CO_2 and CH_4 concentrations far exceed the natural range over the last 650,000 years and have increased markedly (35% and 148% respectively), since the beginning of the industrial era in 1750.

• Both past and future anthropogenic CO_2 emissions will continue to contribute to warming and sea level rise for more than a millennium, due to the time scales required for the removal of the gas from the atmosphere.

- Warming temperatures reduce oceanic uptake of atmospheric CO_2, increasing the fraction of anthropogenic emissions remaining in the atmosphere. This positive carbon cycle feedback results in increasingly greater accumulation of atmospheric CO_2 and subsequently greater warming trends than would otherwise be present in the absence of a feedback relationship.

- There is very high confidence that the global average net effect of human activities since 1750 has been one of warming.

- Scientific evidence shows that major and widespread climate changes have occurred with startling speed. For example, roughly half the north Atlantic warming during the last 20,000 years was achieved in only a decade, and it was accompanied by significant climatic changes across most of the globe (NRC 2008).

What scientists think is likely...

- Anthropogenic warming over the last three decades has likely had a discernible influence at the global scale on observed changes in many physical and biological systems.

- Average temperatures in the Northern Hemisphere during the second half of the 20th century were very likely higher than during any other 50-year period in the last 500 years and likely the highest in at least the past 1300 years.

- Most of the warming that has occurred since the mid-20th century is very likely due to increases in anthropogenic greenhouse gas concentrations. Furthermore, it is extremely likely that global changes observed in the past 50 years can only be explained with external (anthropogenic) forcings (influences) (Figure 2).

- There is much evidence and scientific consensus that greenhouse gas emissions will continue to grow under current climate change mitigation policies and development practices. For the next two decades a warming of about 0.2°C per decade is projected for a range of emissions scenarios; afterwards, temperature projections increasingly depend on specific emissions scenarios (Table 1).

- It is very likely that continued greenhouse gas emissions at or above the current rate will cause further warming and result in changes in the global climate system that will be larger than those observed during the 20th century.

- It is very likely that hot extremes, heat waves and heavy precipitation events will become more frequent. As with current trends, warming is expected to be greatest over land and at most high northern latitudes, and least over the Southern Ocean (near Antarctica) and the northern North Atlantic Ocean.

What scientists think is possible...

- Global temperatures are projected to increase in the future, and the magnitude of temperature change depends on specific emissions scenarios, and ranges from a 1.1°C to 6.4°C increase by 2100 (Table 1).

Table 1. Projected global average surface warming at the end of the 21st century, adapted from (IPCC 2007b).

Notes: a) Temperatures are assessed best estimates and likely uncertainty ranges from a hierarchy of models of varying complexity as well as observational constraints. b) Temperature changes are expressed as the difference from the period 1980-1999. To express the change relative to the period 1850-1899 add 0.5°C. c) Year 2000 constant composition is derived from Atmosphere-Ocean General Circulation Models (AOGCMs) only.

	Temperature Change (°C at 2090 – 2099 relative to 1980 – 1999)[a,b]	
Emissions Scenario	Best Estimate	Likely Range
Constant Year 2000 Concentrations[a]	0.6	0.3 – 0.9
B_1 Scenario	1.8	1.1 – 2.9
B_2 Scenario	2.4	1.4 – 3.8
A_1B Scenario	2.8	1.7 – 4.4
A_2 Scenario	3.4	2.0 – 5.4
A_1F_1 Scenario	4.0	2.4 – 6.4

Figure 3. Sea ice concentrations (the amount of ice in a given area) simulated by the GFDL CM2.1 global coupled climate model averaged over August, September and October (the months when Arctic sea ice concentrations generally are at a minimum). Three years (1885, 1985 & 2085) are shown to illustrate the model-simulated trend. A dramatic reduction of summertime sea ice is projected, with the rate of decrease being greatest during the 21st century portion. The colors range from dark blue (ice free) to white (100% sea ice covered); Image courtesy of NOAA GFDL.

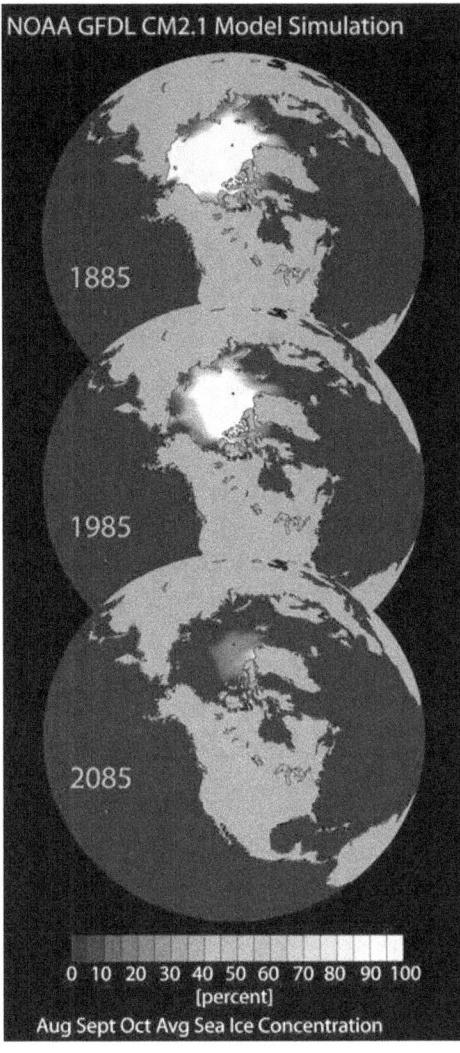

- Anthropogenic warming could lead to changes in the global system that are abrupt and irreversible, depending on the rate and magnitude of climate change.

- Roughly 20-30% of species around the globe could become extinct if global average temperatures increase by 2 to 3°C over pre-industrial levels.

B. Water, Snow, and Ice

What scientists know...

- Many natural systems are already being affected by increased temperatures, particularly those related to snow, ice, and frozen ground. Examples are decreases in snow and ice extent, especially of mountain glaciers; enlargement and increased numbers of glacial lakes; decreased permafrost extent; increasing ground instability in permafrost regions and rock avalanches in mountain regions; and thinner sea ice and shorter freezing seasons of lake and river ice (Figure 3).

- Annual average Arctic sea ice extent has shrunk by 2.7% per decade since 1978, and the summer ice extent has decreased by 7.4% per decade. Sea ice extent during the 2007 melt season plummeted to the lowest levels since satellite measurements began in 1979, and at the end of the melt season September 2007 sea ice was 39% below the long-term (1979-2000) average (NSIDC 2008)(Figure 4).

- Global average sea level rose at an average rate of 1.8 mm per year from 1961 to 2003 and at an average rate of 3.1 mm per year from 1993 to 2003. Increases in sea level since 1993 are the result of the following contributions: thermal expansion, 57%; melting glaciers and ice caps, 28%, melting polar ice sheets, 15%.

- The CO_2 content of the oceans increased by 118 ± 19 Gt (1 Gt = 109 tons) between A.D. 1750 (the end of the pre-industrial period) and 1994 as the result of uptake of anthropogenic CO_2 emissions from the atmosphere, and continues to increase by about 2 Gt each year (Sabine et al. 2004; Hoegh-Guldberg et al. 2007). This

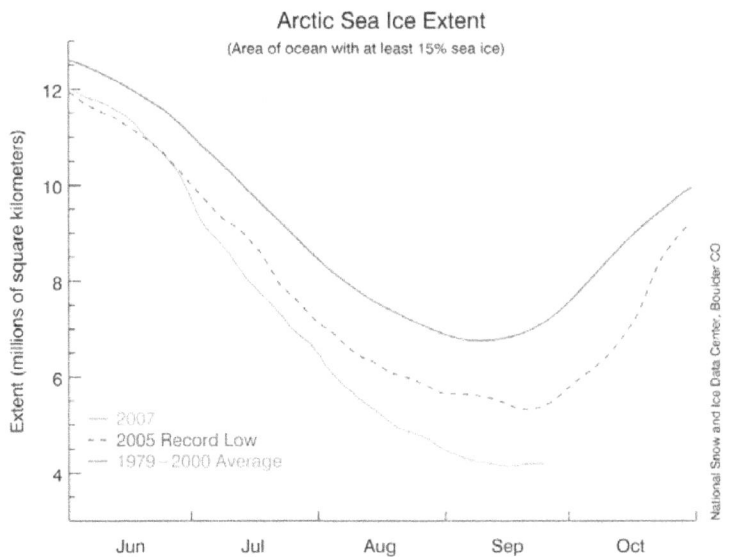

Figure 4. Arctic sea ice in September 2007 (blue line) is far below the previous low record year of 2005 (dashed line), and was 39% below where we would expect to be in an average year (solid gray line). Average September sea ice extent from 1979 to 2000 was 7.04 million square kilometers. The climatological minimum from 1979 to 2000 was 6.74 million square kilometers (NSIDC 2008).

increase in oceanic CO_2 has resulted in a 30% increase in acidity (a decrease in surface ocean pH by an average of 0.1 units), with observed and potential severe negative consequences for marine organisms and coral reef formations (Orr et al. 2005: McNeil and Matear 2007; Riebesell et al. 2009).

• Oceans are noisier due to ocean acidification reducing the ability of seawater to absorb low frequency sounds (noise from ship traffic and military activities). Low-frequency sound absorption has decreased over 10% in both the Pacific and Atlantic over the past 200 years. An assumed additional pH drop of 0.3 (due to anthropogenic CO_2 emissions) accompanied with warming will lead to sound absorption below 1 kHz being reduced by almost half of current values (Hester et. al. 2008).

• Even if greenhouse gas concentrations are stabilized at current levels thermal expansion of ocean waters (and resulting sea level rise) will continue for many centuries, due to the time required to transport heat into the deep ocean.

• Observations since 1961 show that the average global ocean temperature has increased to depths of at least 3000 meters, and that the ocean has been taking up over 80% of the heat added to the climate system.

• Hydrologic effects of climate change include increased runoff and earlier spring peak discharge in many glacier- and snow-fed rivers, and warming of lakes and rivers.

• Runoff is projected to increase by 10 to 40% by mid-century at higher latitudes and in some wet tropical areas, and to decrease by 10 to 30% over some dry regions at mid-latitudes and dry tropics. Areas in which runoff is projected to decline face a reduction in the value of the services provided by water resources.

• Precipitation increased significantly from 1900 to 2005 in eastern parts of North and South America, northern Europe, and northern and central Asia. Conversely, precipitation declined in the Sahel, the Mediterranean, southern Africa, and parts of southern Asia (Figure 5).

What scientists think is likely....

• Widespread mass losses from glaciers and reductions in snow cover are projected to accelerate throughout the 21st century, reducing water availability and changing seasonality of flow patterns.

• Model projections include contraction of snow cover area, widespread increases in depth to frost in permafrost areas, and Arctic and Antarctic sea ice shrinkage.

• The incidence of extreme high sea level has likely increased at a broad range of sites worldwide since 1975.

• Based on current model simulations it is very likely that the meridional overturning circulation (MOC) of the Atlantic Ocean will slow down during the 21st century; nevertheless regional temperatures are predicted to increase. Large-scale and persistent changes in the MOC may result in changes in marine ecosystem productivity,

Figure 5. Relative changes in precipitation (in percent) for the period 2090-2099, relative to 1980-1999. Values are multi-model averages based on the SRES A₁B scenario for December to February (left) and June to August (right). White areas are where less than 66% of the models agree in the sign of the change and stippled areas are where more than 90% of the models agree in the sign of the change (IPCC 2007a).

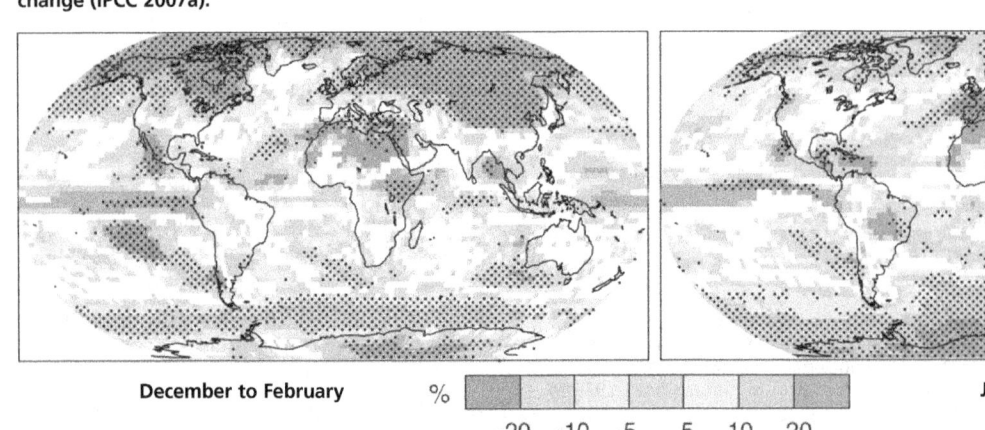

December to February   %   -20   -10   -5   5   10   20   June to August

Table 2. Projected global average sea level rise at the end of the 21st century, adapted from IPCC 2007b.

Notes: a) Temperatures are assessed best estimates and likely uncertainty ranges from a hierarchy of models of varying complexity as well as observational constraints.

Emissions Scenario	Sea level rise (m at 2090 – 2099 relative to 1980 – 1999)
	Model-based range (excluding future rapid dynamical changes in ice flow)
Constant Year 2000 Concentrations[a]	0.3 – 0.9
B_1 Scenario	1.1 – 2.9
B_2 Scenario	1.4 – 3.8
A_1B Scenario	1.7 – 4.4
A_2 Scenario	2.0 – 5.4
A_1F_1 Scenario	2.4 – 6.4

fisheries, ocean CO_2 uptake, and terrestrial vegetation.

- Globally the area affected by drought has likely increased since the 1970s and the frequency of extreme precipitation events has increased over most areas.

- Future tropical cyclones (typhoons and hurricanes) are likely to become more intense, with larger peak wind speeds and increased heavy precipitation. Extra-tropical storm tracks are projected to move poleward, with consequent shifts in wind, precipitation, and temperature patterns.

- Increases in the amount of precipitation are very likely in high latitudes and decreases are likely in most subtropical land regions, continuing observed patterns (Figure 5).

- Increases in the frequency of heavy precipitation events in the coming century are very likely, resulting in potential damage to crops and property, soil erosion, surface and groundwater contamination, and increased risk of human death and injury.

What scientists think is possible...

- Arctic late-summer sea ice may disappear almost entirely by the end of the 21st century (Figure 3).

- Current global model studies project that the Antarctic ice sheet will remain too cold for widespread surface melting and gain mass due to increased snowfall. However, net loss of ice mass could occur if dynami-

cal ice discharge dominates the ice sheet mass balance.

- Model-based projections of global average sea level rise at the end of the 21st century range from 0.18 to 0.59 meters, depending on specific emissions scenarios (Table 2). These projections may actually underestimate future sea level rise because they do not include potential feedbacks or full effects of changes in ice sheet flow.

- Partial loss of ice sheets and/or the thermal expansion of seawater over very long time scales could result in meters of sea level rise, major changes in coastlines and inundation of low-lying areas, with greatest effects in river deltas and low-lying islands.

C. Vegetation and Wildlife

What scientists know...

- Temperature increases have affected Arctic and Antarctic ecosystems and predator species at high levels of the food web.

- Changes in water temperature, salinity, oxygen levels, circulation, and ice cover in marine and freshwater ecosystems have resulted in shifts in ranges and changes in algal, plankton, and fish abundance in high-latitude oceans; increases in algal and zooplankton abundance in high-latitude and high-altitude lakes; and range shifts and earlier fish migrations in rivers.

- High-latitude (cooler) ocean waters are currently acidified enough to start dissolving pteropods; open water marine snails which are one of the primary food sources of young salmon and mackerel (Fabry et al. 2008, Feely et al. 2008). In lower latitude (warmer) waters, by the end of this century Humboldt squid's metabolic rate will be reduced by 31% and activity levels by 45% due to reduced pH, leading to squid retreating at night to shallower waters to feed and replenish oxygen levels (Rosa and Seibel 2008).

- A meta-analysis of climate change effects on range boundaries in Northern Hemisphere species of birds, butterflies, and alpine herbs shows an average shift of 6.1 kilometers per decade northward (or 6.1 meters per decade upward), and a mean shift toward earlier onset of spring events (frog breeding, bird nesting, first flowering, tree budburst, and arrival of migrant butterflies and birds) of 2.3 days per decade (Parmesan and Yohe 2003).

- Poleward range shifts of individual species and expansions of warm-adapted communities have been documented on all continents and in most of the major oceans of the world (Parmesan 2006).

- Satellite observations since 1980 indicate a trend in many regions toward earlier greening of vegetation in the spring linked to longer thermal growing seasons resulting from recent warming.

- Over the past 50 years humans have changed ecosystems more rapidly and extensively than in any previous period of human history, primarily as the result of growing demands for food, fresh water, timber, fiber, and fuel. This has resulted in a substantial and largely irreversible loss of Earth's biodiversity

- Although the relationships have not been quantified, it is known that loss of intact ecosystems results in a reduction in ecosystem services (clean water, carbon sequestration, waste decomposition, crop pollination, etc.).

What scientists think is likely...

- The resilience of many ecosystems is likely to be exceeded this century by an unprecedented combination of climate change, associated disturbance (flooding, drought, wildfire, insects, ocean acidification) and other global change drivers (land use change, pollution, habitat fragmentation, invasive species, resource over-exploitation) (Figure 6).

- Exceedance of ecosystem resilience may be characterized by threshold-type responses such as extinctions, disruption of ecological interactions, and major changes in ecosystem structure and disturbance regimes.

- Net carbon uptake by terrestrial ecosystems is likely to peak before mid-century and then weaken or reverse, amplifying climate changes. By 2100 the terrestrial biosphere is likely to become a carbon source.

- Increases in global average temperature above 1.5 to 2.5°C and concurrent atmospheric CO_2 concentrations are projected to result in major changes in ecosystem structure and function, species' ecological interactions, and species' geographical ranges. Negative consequences are projected for species biodiversity and ecosystem goods and services.

- Model projections for increased atmospheric CO_2 concentration and global temperatures significantly exceed values for at least the past 420,000 years, the period during which more extant marine organisms evolved. Under expected 21st century conditions it is likely that global warming and ocean acidification will compromise carbonate accretion, resulting in less diverse reef communities and failure of some existing carbonate reef structures. Climate changes will likely exacerbate local stresses from declining water quality and overexploitation of key species (Hoegh-Guldberg et al. 2007).

- Ecosystems likely to be significantly impacted by changing climatic conditions include:

  i. Terrestrial – tundra, boreal forest, and mountain regions (sensitivity to warming); Mediterranean-type ecosystems and tropical rainforests (decreased rainfall)

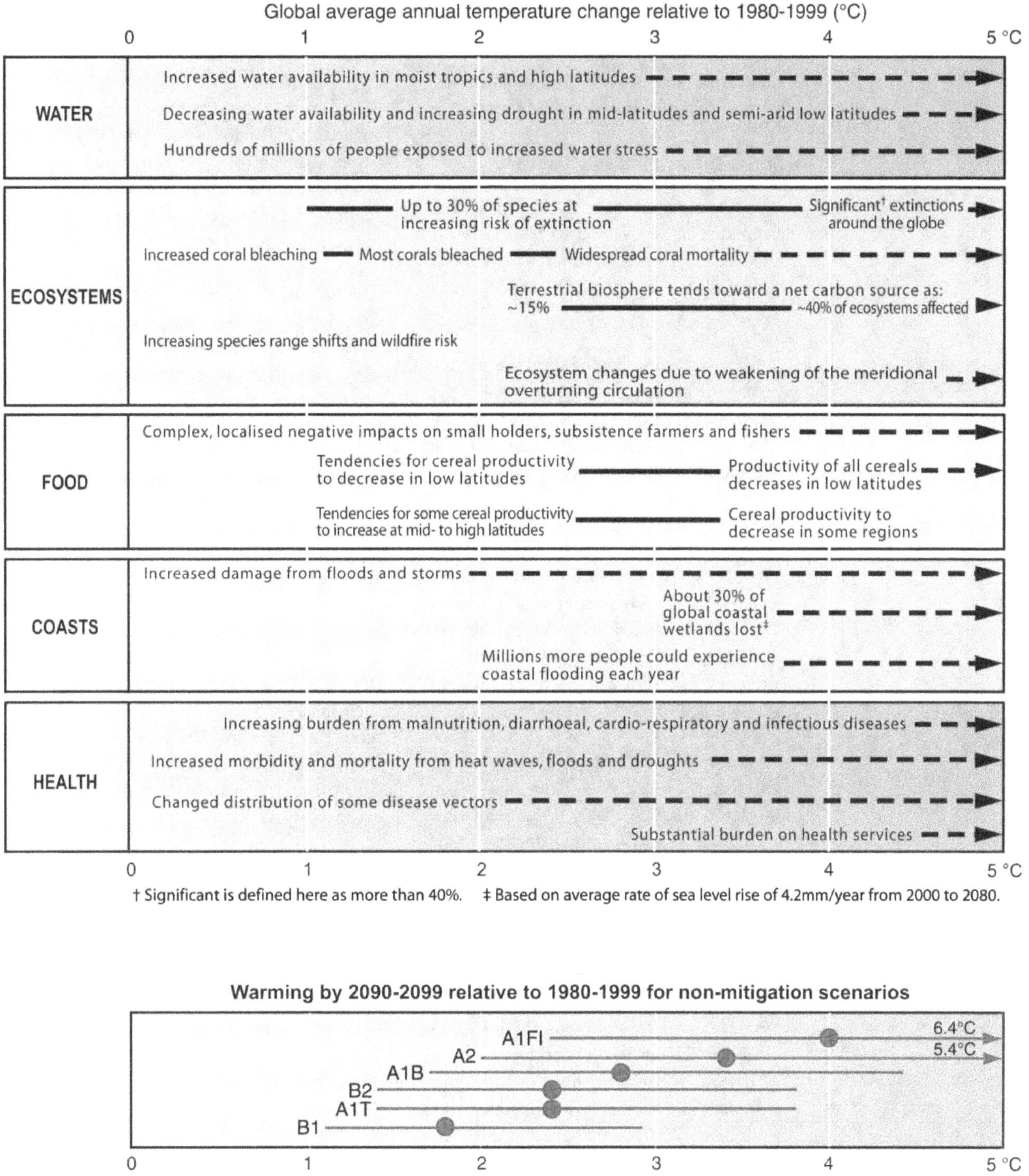

Global average annual temperature change relative to 1980-1999 (°C)

| | 0 | 1 | 2 | 3 | 4 | 5 °C |

WATER

Increased water availability in moist tropics and high latitudes ──────────▶

Decreasing water availability and increasing drought in mid-latitudes and semi-arid low latitudes ───▶

Hundreds of millions of people exposed to increased water stress ──────────▶

ECOSYSTEMS

Up to 30% of species at increasing risk of extinction ───── Significant† extinctions around the globe ▶

Increased coral bleaching ── Most corals bleached ── Widespread coral mortality ──────▶

Terrestrial biosphere tends toward a net carbon source as:
~15% ───────── ~40% of ecosystems affected ▶

Increasing species range shifts and wildfire risk

Ecosystem changes due to weakening of the meridional overturning circulation ─▶

FOOD

Complex, localised negative impacts on small holders, subsistence farmers and fishers ──────▶

Tendencies for cereal productivity to decrease in low latitudes ───── Productivity of all cereals decreases in low latitudes ─▶

Tendencies for some cereal productivity to increase at mid- to high latitudes ───── Cereal productivity to decrease in some regions

COASTS

Increased damage from floods and storms ──────────▶

About 30% of global coastal wetlands lost‡ ────▶

Millions more people could experience coastal flooding each year ────▶

HEALTH

Increasing burden from malnutrition, diarrhoeal, cardio-respiratory and infectious diseases ──▶

Increased morbidity and mortality from heat waves, floods and droughts ──────────▶

Changed distribution of some disease vectors ──────────────▶

Substantial burden on health services ───▶

| | 0 | 1 | 2 | 3 | 4 | 5 °C |

† Significant is defined here as more than 40%.   ‡ Based on average rate of sea level rise of 4.2mm/year from 2000 to 2080.

Warming by 2090-2099 relative to 1980-1999 for non-mitigation scenarios

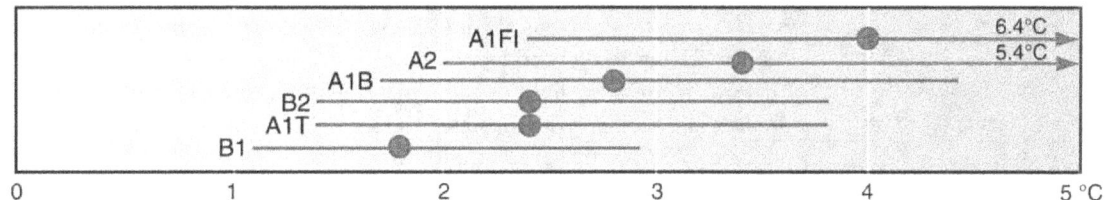

| | 0 | 1 | 2 | 3 | 4 | 5 °C |

A1FI ──────────── 6.4°C
A2 ──────────── 5.4°C
A1B ────────────
B2 ────────────
A1T ────────────
B1 ────────────

Figure 6. Examples of impacts associated with projected global average surface warming. Upper panel: Illustrative examples of global impacts projected for climate changes (and sea level and atmospheric CO_2 where relevant) associated with different amounts of increase in global average surface temperature in the 21st century. The black lines link impacts; broken-line arrows indicate impacts continuing with increasing temperature. Entries are placed so that the left-hand side of text indicates the approximate level of warming that is associated with the onset of a given impact. Quantitative entries for water scarcity and flooding represent the additional impacts of climate change relative to the conditions projected across the range of SRES scenarios A1FI, A2, B1 and B2. Adaptation to climate change is not included in these estimations. Confidence levels for all statements are high. Lower panel: Dots and bars indicate the best estimate and likely ranges of warming assessed for the six SRES marker scenarios for 2090-2099 relative to 1980-1999 (IPCC 2007a).

ii. Coastal – mangroves and salt marshes (multiple stresses)

iii. Marine – coral reefs (multiple stresses); sea-ice biomes (sensitivity to warming)

What scientists think is possible...

- Approximately 20% to 30% of plant and animal species assessed to date are at increased risk of extinction with increases in global average temperature in excess of 1.5 to 2.5°C.

- Endemic species may be more vulnerable to climate changes, and therefore at higher risk for extinction, because they may have evolved in locations where paleo-climatic conditions have been stable.

- Although there is great uncertainty about how forests will respond to changing climate and increasing levels of atmospheric CO_2, the factors that are most typically predicted to influence forests are increased fire, increased drought, and greater vulnerability to insects and disease (Brown 2008).

- If atmospheric CO_2 levels reach 450 ppm (projected to occur by 2030–2040 at the current emissions rates), reefs may experience rapid and terminal decline worldwide from multiple climate change-related direct and indirect effects including mass bleaching, ocean acidification, damage to shallow reef communities,reduction of biodiversity, and extinctions. (Veron et al. 2009). At atmospheric CO_2 levels of 560 ppmv, calcification of tropical corals is expected to decline by 30%, and loss of coral structure in areas of high erosion may outpace coral growth. With unabated CO_2 emissions, 70% of the presently known reef locations (including cold-water corals) will be in corrosive waters by the end of this century (Riebesell, et al. 2009).

D. Disturbance

What scientists know...

- Climate change currently contributes to the global burden of disease and premature death through exposure to extreme events and changes in water and air quality, food quality and quantity, ecosystems, agriculture, and economy (Parry et al. 2007).

- The most vulnerable industries, settlements, and societies are generally those in coastal and river flood plains, those whose economies are closely linked with climate-sensitive resources, and those in areas prone to extreme weather events.

- By 2080-2090 millions more people than today are projected to experience flooding due to sea level rise, especially those in the low-lying megadeltas of Asia and Africa and on small islands.

- Climate change affects the function and operation of existing water infrastructure and water management practices, aggravating the impacts of population growth, changing economic activity, land-use change, and urbanization.

What scientists think is likely...

- Up to 20% of the world's population will live in areas where river flood potential could increase by 2080-2090, with major consequences for human health, physical infrastructure, water quality, and resource availability.

- The health status of millions of people is projected to be affected by climate change, through increases in malnutrition; increased deaths, disease, and injury due to extreme weather events; increased burden of diarrheal diseases; increased cardio-respiratory disease due to higher concentrations of ground-level ozone in urban areas; and altered spatial distribution of vector-borne diseases.

- Risk of hunger is projected to increase at lower latitudes, especially in seasonally dry and tropical regions.

What scientists think is possible...

- Although many diseases are projected to increase in scope and incidence as the result of climate changes, lack of appropriate longitudinal data on climate change-related health impacts precludes definitive assessment.

V. References

Aeby, G., T. Work, D. Fenner and E. Didonato (2007). Coral and crustose coralline algae disease on the reefs of American Samoa. Proceedings of the 11th International Coral Reef Symposium. Ft. Lauderdale, Florida.

Amelung, B., S. Nicholls and D. Viner (2007). "Implications of global climate change for tourism flows and seasonality." Journal of Travel Research 45(3):285.

Anderson, C. L. (2009). Gendered dimensions of disaster risk management, natural resource management, and climate change adaptation in the Paci!c. Women in Fisheries Information Bulletin. V. Vuki, Secretariat of the Pacific Community. 20:7.

Andersson, A. J., I. B. Kuffner, F. T. Mackenzie, P. L. Jokiel, K. S. Rodgers and A. Tan (2009). "Net Loss of CaCO3 from a subtropical calcifying community due to seawater acidification: mesocosm-scale experimental evidence." Biogeosciences 6(8): 1811-1823.

Antonelis, G. A., J. D. Baker, T. C. Johanos, R. C. Braun and A. L. Harting (2006). "Hawaiian monk seal (Monachus schauinslandi): Status and conservation issues." Atoll Research Bulletin 543: 75-101.

Atkinson, C. T. and D. A. LaPointe (2009). "Introduced Avian Diseases, Climate Change, and the Future of Hawaiian Honeycreepers." Journal of Avian Medicine and Surgery 23(1): 53-63.

Baker, J. and T. C. Johanos (2004). "Abundance of the Hawaiian monk seal in the main Hawaiian Islands." Biological Conservation 116: 103–110.

Baker, J. D., C. L. Littnan and D. W. Johnston (2006). "Potential effects of sea level rise on the terrestrial habitats of endangered and endemic megafauna in the Northwestern Hawaiian Islands." Endangered Species Research 4: 1-10.

Benning, T. L., D. LaPointe, C. T. Atkinson and P. M. Vitousek (2002). "Interactions of climate change with biological invasions and land use in the Hawaiian Islands: Modeling the fate of endemic birds using a geographic information system." PNAS 99(2): 14246–14249.

Bettencourt, S., R. Croad, P. Freeman, J. Hay, R. Jones, P. King, P. Lal, A. Mearns, G. Miller, I. Pswarayi-Riddihough, A. Simpson, N. Teuatabo, U. Trotz and M. Van Aalst (2006). Not If But When: Adapting to Natural Hazards In the Pacific Islands Region, The World Bank: 46.

Brown, R. (2008). The implications of climate change for conservation, restoration, and management of National Forest lands. National Forest Restoration Collaborative.

Burdick, D., V. Brown, J. Asher, C. Caballes, M. Gawel, L. Goldman, A. Hall, J. Kenyon, T. Leberer, E., J. M. Lundblad, J. Miller, D. Minton, M. Nadon, N. Pioppi, L. Raymundo, B. Richards, R. Schroeder, P. Schupp, E. Smith and B. Zgliczynski (2008). Status of the Coral Reef Ecosystems of Guam, Bureau of Statistics and Plans, Guam Coastal Management Program: iv + 76.

Caldeira, K. (2007). "What Corals are Dying to Tell Us About CO2 and Ocean Acidification." Oceanography 20(2): 188-195.

Cao, G., T. W. Giambelluca, D. E. Stevens and T. A. Schroeder (2007). "Inversion Variability in the Hawaiian Trade Wind Regime." Journal of Climate 20(7): 1145-1160.

CCSP (2008). Weather and Climate Extremes in a Changing Climate. Regions of Focus: North America, Hawaii, Caribbean, and U.S. Pacific Islands. A Report by the U.S. Climate Change Science Program and the Subcommittee on Global Change Research. . T. R. Karl, Gerald A. Meehl, Christopher D. Miller, Susan J. Hassol, Anne M. Waple, and William L. Murray Washington, D.C., USA, Department of Commerce, NOAA's National Climatic Data Center: 164.

Cesar, H. S. F. and P. F. H. van Beukering (2004). "Economic Valuation of the Coral Reefs of Hawai'i." Pacific Science Volume 58(2): 231-242.

Chen, J. L., C. R. Wilson, B. D. Tapley and X. G. Hu (2006). "Thermosteric effects on interannual and long-term global mean sea level changes." Journal of Geodesy 80(5): 240-247.

Diaz, H. F., P.-S. Chu and J. K. Eischeid (2005). Rainfall changes in Hawaii during the last century. 16th Conference on Climate Variability and Change, Boston, MA, American Meteorological Society.

Emanuel, K., R. Sundararajan and J. Williams (2007). "Hurricanes and Global Warming: Results from Downscaling IPCC AR4 Simulations." Bulletin of the American Meteorological Society 89: 347-367.

Fabry, V. J, B. A. Seibel, R. A. Feely, and J. C. Orr (2008). Impacts of ocean acidification on marine fauna and ecosystem processes. ICES Journal of Marine Science 65: 414-432.

Feely, R. A., C. L. Sabine, J. M. Hernandez-Ayon, D. Lanson and B. Hales (2008). Evidence for upwelling of corrosive "acidified" water onto the continental shelf. Science 320(5882): 1490-1492.

Field, M. E., S. A. Cochran, J. B. Logan and C. D. Storlazzi Eds. (2008). The coral reef of south Moloka'i, Hawai'i — portrait of a sediment-threatened fringing reef. U.S. Geological Survey Scientific Investigations Report 2007-5101.

Finucane, M. L. (2009). Why Science Alone Won't Solve the Climate Crisis: Managing Climate Risks in the Pacific. Asia Pacific Issues. 89: 8.

Fletcher, C. H. (2009). "Sea level by the end of the 21st century: A review." Shore & Beach 77(4): 4-12.

Fletcher, C. H., E. E. Grossman, B. M. Richmond and A. E. Gibbs (2002). Atlas of Natural Hazards in the Hawaiian Coastal Zone, U.S. Geological Survey. Geologic Investigations Series I-2761: 182.

Foster, P. (2001). "The potential negative impacts of global climate change on tropical montane cloud forests." Earth-Science Reviews 55: 73–106.

Freed, L. A., R. L. Cann, M. L. Goff, W. A. Kuntz and G. R. Bodner (2005). "Increase in avian malaria at upper elevation in Hawai'i." The Condor 107(4): 753-764.

Füssel, H.-M. (2009). "An updated assessment of the risks from climate change based on research published since the IPCC Fourth Assessment Report." Climatic Change 97: 469-482.

Giambelluca, T. W., H. F. Diaz and M. S. A. Luke (2008). "Secular temperature changes in Hawai'i." Geophysical Research Letters 35: L12702.

Gilman, E. L., J. Ellison, N. C. Duke and C. Field (2008). "Threats to mangroves from climate change and adaptation options: A review." Aquatic Botany 89(2): 237-250.

Gilman, E. L., J. Ellison, I. Sauni Jr. and S. Tuaumu (2007). "Trends in surface elevations of American Samoa mangroves." Wetlands Ecology Management 15: 391–404.

Gilman, E., J. Ellison and R. Coleman (2006). "Assessment of Mangrove Response to Projected Relative Sea-Level Rise And Recent Historical Reconstruction of Shoreline Position " Environmental Monitoring and Assessment 124(1-3): 105-130.

Gingerich, S. B., C. W. Yeung, T-J. N. Ibarra and J. A. Engott (2007). Water Use in Wetland Kalo Cultivation in Hawai'i, U.S. Geological Survey Open-File Report 2007–1157: 68.

Guinotte, J. M., R. W. Buddemeier and J. A. Kleypas (2003). "Future coral reef habitat marginality: temporal and spatial effects of climate change in the Pacific basin." Coral Reefs 22(4): 551-558.

Harvell, C. D., C. E. Mitchell, J. R. Ward, S. Altizer, A. P. Dobson, R. S. Ostfeld and M. D. Samuel (2002). "Climate Warming and Disease Risk for Terrestrial and Marine Biota." Science 296(5576): 2158-2162.

Hester, K. C., E. T. Peltzer, W. J. Kirkwood and P. G. Brewer (2008). "Unanticipated consequences of ocean acidification: A noisier ocean at lower pH." Geophysical Research Letters 35: L19601.

Hoegh-Guldberg, O., P. J. Mumby, A. J. Hooten, R. S. Steneck, P. Greenfield, E. Gomez, C. D. Harvell, P. F. Sale, A. J. Edwards, K. Caldeira, N. Knowlton, C. M. Eakin, R. Iglesias-Prieto, N. Muthiga, R. H. Bradbury, A. Dubi and M. E. Hatziolos (2007). "Coral Reefs Under Rapid Climate Change and Ocean Acidification." Science 318: 1737-1742.

Hughes, T. P., A. H. Baird, D. R. Bellwood, M. Card, S. R. Connolly, C. Folke, R. Grosberg, O. Hoegh-Guldberg, J. B. C. Jackson, J. Kleypas, J. M. Lough, P. Marshall, M. Nystrom, S. R. Palumbi, J. M. Pandolfi, B. Rosen and J. Roughgarden (2003). "Climate Change, Human Impacts, and the Resilience of Coral Reefs." Science 301: 929-933.

ICAP (2010). Hawaii's Changing Climate. D. o. G. a. G. Dr. Chip Fletcher. Honolulu, HI, School of Ocean and Earth Science and Technology, University of Hawai'i at Mänoa: 6.

IPCC (2007). Climate Change 2007: Impacts, Adaptation and Vulnerability. Contribution of Working Group II to the Fourth Assessment Report of the Intergovernmental Panel on Climate Change. O. F. C. M.L. Parry, J.P. Palutikof, P.J. van der Linden, C.E. Hanson. Cambridge, UK: 976.

IPCC. (2007a). Climate Change 2007: Synthesis Report. Contribution of Working Groups I, II, and III to the Fourth Assessment Report of the Intergovernmental Panel on Climate Change. [Core Writing Team, Pachauri, R.K and Reisinger, A. (eds.)]. IPCC, Geneva, Switzerland, 104 pp.

IPCC. (2007b). Climate Change 2007: The Physical Science Basis. Contribution of Working Group I to the Fourth Assessment Report of the Intergovernmental Panel on Climate Change [Solomon, S., D. Qin, M. Manning, Z. Chen, M. Marquis, K.B. Averyt, M. Tignor and H.L. Miller (eds.)]. Cambridge University Press, Cambridge, United Kingdom and New York, NY, USA, 996 pp.

Jokiel, P. L., Ed. (2008). Biology and Ecological Functioning of Coral Reefs in the Main Hawaiian Islands, in Coral Reefs of the USA. Coral Reefs of the World, Springer Netherlands.

Jokiel, P. L., K. S. Rodgers, I. B. Kuffner, A. J. Andersson, E. F. Cox and F. T. Mackenzie (2008). "Ocean acidification and calcifying reef organisms: a mesocosm investigation." Coral Reefs 27(473-483).

Jokiel, P. L. and E. K. Brown (2004). "Global warming, regional trends and inshore environmental conditions influence coral bleaching in Hawaii." Global Change Biology 10: 1627–1641.

Kleypas, J. (2006). Predictions of Climate Change in the Tropical Oceans, and How That Should Shape our Conservation Efforts. World Maritime Technology Conference.

Kleypas, J. A., R. A. Feely, V. J. Fabry, C. Langdon, C. L. Sabine and L. L. Robbins (2006). Impacts of Ocean Acidification on Coral Reefs and Other Marine Calcifiers: A Guide for Future Research. report of a workshop. St. Petersburg, FL, NSF, NOAA, U.S. Geological Survey: 88.

Kleypas, J. A., R. W. Buddemeier, D. Archer, J-P. Gattuso, C. Langdon and B. N. Opdyke (1999). "Geochemical Consequences of Increased Atmospheric Carbon Dioxide on Coral Reefs." Science 284: 118-120.

Kruk, M. C. and D. H. Levinson (2008). Evaluating the Impacts of Climate Change on Rainfall Extremes for Hawaii and Coastal Alaska. The 24th Conference on Severe Local Storms.

Lal, P. N., J. Kinch and F. Wickham (2009). Review of Economic and Livelihood Impact Assessments of, and Adaptation to, Climate Change in Melanesia Secretariat of the Pacific Regional Environment Programme.

Lean, J. L. and D. H. Rind (2009). "How will Earth's surface temperature change in future decades?" Geophysical Research Letters 36: L15708.

Lebrato, M., D. Iglesias-Rodriguez, R. Feely, D. Greeley, D. Jones, N. Suarez-Bosche, R. Lampitt, J. Cartes, D. Green and B. Alker (2009: preprint). "Global contribution of echinoderms to the marine carbon cycle: a re-assessment of the oceanic $CaCO_3$ budget and the benthic compartments." Ecological Monographs 0(0).

McNeil, B. I. and R. J. Matear. (2007). Climate change feedbacks on future oceanic acidification. Tellus 59B: 191–198.

NABCI (2010). The State of the Birds 2010 Report on Climate Change United States. The State of the Birds. A. F. King. Washington, DC, Department of the Interior, North American Bird Conservation Initiative.

NRC (2008). Ecological impacts of climate change. The National Academies Press, Washington, D.C.

NSIDC (2008). National Snow and Ice Data Center.

Nadkarni, N. M. and R. Solano (2002). "Potential Effects of Climate Change on Canopy Communities in a Tropical Cloud Forest: An Experimental Approach." Oecologia 131(4): 580-586.

Oki, D. S. (2004). Trends in Streamflow Characteristics in Hawaii, 1913–2002, U.S. Geological Survey Fact Sheet 2004-3104: 4.

Orr, J. C., V. J. Fabry, O. Aumont, L. Bopp, S. C. Doney, R. A. Feely, A. Gnanadesikan, N. Gruber, A. Ishida and F. Joos. (2005). Anthropogenic ocean acidification over the twenty-first century and its impact on calcifying organisms. Nature 437(29): 681-686.

Parmesan, C. (2006). "Ecological and Evolutionary Responses to Recent Climate Change." Annual Review of Ecology, Evolution and Systematics 37: 637-669.

Parmesan, C. and G. Yohe (2003). "A globally coherent fingerprint of climate change impacts across natural systems." Nature 421: 37-42.

Parry, M. L., O. F. Canziani, J. P. Palutikof, and Co-authors (2007): Technical Summary. Climate Change 2007: Impacts, Adaptation and Vulnerability. Contribution of Working Group II to the Fourth Assessment Report of the Intergovernmental Panel on Climate Change, M.L. Parry, O.F. Canziani, J.P. Palutikof, P.J. van der Linden and C.E. Hanson, Eds., Cambridge University Press, Cambridge, UK, 23-78.

Pendleton, E. A., E. R. Thieler and S. J. Williams (2010). "Importance of Coastal Change Variables in Determining Vulnerability to Sea- and Lake-Level Change." Journal of Coastal Research 26(1): 176-183.

Polovina, J. J. (2005). "Climate variation, regime shifts, and implications for sustainable fisheries." Bulletin of Marine Science 76(2): 233-244.

Polovina, J. J., E. A. Howell and M. Abecassis (2008). "Ocean's least productive waters are expanding." Geophysical Research Letters 35: L03618.

Riebesell, U., A. Kortzinger and A. Oschlies. (2009). Sensitivities of marine carbon fluxes to ocean change. Proceedings of the National Academy of Sciences 106(49): 20602–20609.

RÖdder, D. (2009). "'Sleepless in Hawaii' – does anthropogenic climate change enhance ecological and socioeconomic impacts of the alien invasive Eleutherodactylus coqui Thomas 1966 (Anura: Eleutherodactylidae)?" North-Western Journal of Zoology 5(1): 16-25.

Root, T. L., J. Price, K. R. Hall, S. H. Schneider, C. Rosenzweig and J. A. Pounds (2003). "Fingerprints of global warming on wild animals and plants." Nature 421: 57-60.

Rosa, R. and B. A. Seibel (2008). Synergistic effects of climate-related variables suggest future physiological impairment in a top oceanic predator. PNAS 105(52): 20776-20780.

Sabine, C. L., R. A. Feely, N. Gruber, R. M. Key, K. Lee, J. L. Bullister, R. Wanninkhof, C. S. Wong, D. W. R. Wallace, B. Tilbrook, F. J. Millero, T.-H. Peng, A. Kozyr, T. Ono and A. F. Rios (2004). The Oceanic Sink for Anthropogenic CO2. 2004 305: 367-371.

Saunders, S., T. Easley and S. Farver; The Rocky Mountain Climate Organization, Contributing Authors, J. A. Logan and T. Spencer (2009). National Parks in Peril: The Threat of Climate Disruption, Rocky Mountain Climate Organization: 56.

Spennemann, D. H. R. (2004). Conservation management and mitigation of the impact of tropical cyclones on archaeological sites. Disaster Management Programs for Historic Sites. D. H. R. Spennemann and D. W. Look. San Francisco and Albury, Association for Preservation Technology (Western Chapter) and The Johnstone Centre, Charles Sturt University: 113-132.

Timm, O. and H. F. Diaz (2009). "Synoptic-Statistical Approach to Regional Downscaling of IPCC Twenty-First-Century Climate Projections: Seasonal Rainfall over the Hawaiian Islands." Journal of Climate 22: 4261-4280.

USGCRP (2009). Global Climate Change Impacts in the United States. T. R. Karl, Jerry M. Melillo, and Thomas C. Peterson, United States Global Change Research Program.

Veron, J. E. N., O. Hoegh-Guldberg, T. M. Lenton, J. M. Lough, D. O. Obura, P. Pearce-Kelly, C. R. C. Sheppard, M. Spalding, M. G. Stafford-Smith and A. D. Rogers (2009). The coral reef crisis: The critical importance of <350 ppm CO2. Marine Pollution Bulletin 58: 1428–1436.

Vitousek, S., M. M. Barbee, C.H. Fletcher, B. M. Richmond and A. S. Genz (2009). Pu'ukoho'o Heiau National Historic Site and Kaloko- Honokohau Historical Park, Big Island of Hawai'i Coastal Hazard Analysis Report, National Park Service: 99.

Waddell, J. E. and A. M. Clarke Eds. (2008). The State of Coral Reef Ecosystems of the United States and Pacific Freely Associated States: 2008. NOAA Technical Memorandum NOS NCCOS 73 Silver Spring, MD, NOAA/NCCOS Center for Coastal Monitoring and Assessment's Biogeography Team.

The Department of the Interior protects and manages the nation's natural resources and cultural heritage; provides scientific and other information about those resources; and honors its special responsibilities to American Indians, Alaska Natives, and affiliated Island Communities.

NPS 963/106399, January 2011

www.ingramcontent.com/pod-product-compliance
Lightning Source LLC
Chambersburg PA
CBHW080932290526
45795CB00007BA/2723